MAKE GOD'S LOVE GO VIRAL!

Copyright © 2024 Gordon Hickson
c/o Heartcry for Change

CMS House I Watlington Road I Oxford I OX4 6BZ I UK
All rights reserved under International Copyright Law. Contents and/or cover may not be reproduced or transmitted in whole or in part, in any form or by any means, electronic or mechanical, including photocopy, recording or any information storage and retrieval system, without express written consent of Gordon Hickson.

A Publication by Gordon Hickson
c/o CMS House I Watlington Road I Oxford I OX4 6BZ
ISBN: 9798326562845

MAKE GOD'S LOVE GO VIRAL!
Activating "the heavenly virus" of God's Kingdom
through understanding Christ's Cross.
by Gordon Hickson

Unless otherwise stated, Scripture quotations are taken from the New International Version of the Bible NIV Copyright 1973,1978, 1984, 2011 by Biblica Inc. Used by permission. All rights reserved worldwide.

Book cover and content layout designed by Ronald Gabrielsen

First edition - Published and printed in June 2024

MAKE GOD'S LOVE GO VIRAL!

Activating "the heavenly virus"
of God's Kingdom through
understanding Christ's cross

GORDON HICKSON

WHAT OTHERS SAY

What sets this book apart from others is Gordon's genuine and infectious passion for spreading God's love. His words leap off the page and into your heart, igniting a fire within you to make a difference in the world. It's impossible not to be moved by his words and the profound impact they can have on your life. In a world filled with negativity and division, this is a beacon of hope and inspiration - a must-read for anyone seeking to make a difference and spread God's love in a world that so desperately needs it. (For full text, see the postscript at the end of the book.)

– Pastor Surprise Sithole
Founding Member and International Director of Pastors for Iris Ministries

The sacrifice and victory of Jesus Christ is the crux of our faith. As followers of Jesus, we never graduate from needing a continual revelation of the Cross. The apostle Paul exhorts us never to stray from the "simplicity and purity of devotion to Christ" (2 Cor. 11:3). In this book, Gordon Hickson passionately unpacks the simplicity and power of the gospel message. I admire the way that he and his wife walk this message out with a genuine love that inspires others to do the same. I am excited about this book, as I believe it carries an impartation that will empower each of us to demonstrate the heart of a loving Father to those around us.

– Bill Johnson
Bethel Church, Redding, CA;
Author of When Heaven Invades Earth and Born for Significance

Jesus Christ is serious about building His Church (Matt 16:18). In this crucial season, a wakeup call is reverberating around the globe, calling believers everywhere to truly be the Church—God's called-out ones. This is our moment to resolve to pray and take action to advance God's Kingdom like never before. Do you want to be a super-spreader of revival? Take this book to heart and join in the Holy Spirit movement.

> **– Dr. Ché Ahn**
> *Senior Leader, Harvest Rock Church, Pasadena, CA;*
> *President, Harvest International Ministry;*
> *International Chancellor, Wagner University*

Gordon's latest book is the most comprehensive and well-balanced teaching on the Cross of Christ that I have come across. Having been involved in Christian ministry for over 62 years and having read numerous books with similar themes, I found this book to be incredibly captivating. Once I started reading, I couldn't put it down until I reached the last page. For those seeking to live a victorious life over the flesh and carnal nature, desiring a fresh Holy Spirit revival and the fulfillment of the mission mandate, this book is a must-read.

> **– Pastor Dennis Balcombe**
> *Revival Chinese Ministries International, Hong Kong SAR*

Are you ready to have your eyes opened and a fresh hunger for God released in you? Then read this book! At this time Jesus is confronting the church in the West with our spiritual blindness and inviting us to have fresh eyes to see the wonders of the life in his Kingdom that he won for us. Gordon has wonderfully captured so much of what Jesus is calling us to see and given us ways to respond through rich insights about the power of the Cross. With stories from his own life and the worldwide church, you will be inspired to step forward with courage and faith to live an abundant life in Christ and make his love known.

– Revd Canon John McGinley
Leader of the Myriad Church Planting Ministry
Overseer of The SEND U.K & Ireland

This book springs from a deep desire in Gordon's heart to see an awakening and revival that will usher in the greatest harvest of souls we have yet known. You will be challenged to re-examine your own heart and attitudes through the fresh revelation of the Cross that Gordon shares in his book. This book has greatly impacted me personally and I know it will you too, as you open your heart to these truths.

– Diane M. Fink
Rev 22.2 Ministries International

Gordon's own life experience of the Kingdom of God as a life-transforming, mission-empowering reality, underlies his keen perceptions of Jesus' core teaching being like a "heavenly virus". Understanding the Cross, as he so rightly claims, can liberate us from bondage to our own egotistical impulses, enabling us to take part in the excitement and fulfillment of the "Jesus Kingdom culture" the Holy Spirit is seeking to spread worldwide. Gordon's deep and at times fiery personal encounters with the Lord, especially regarding reaching others with God's love and in particular those in the Muslim world, have led him to issue this stirring challenge to Christian leaders that I also heartily endorse as an old but "refired" missionary/evangelist myself.

– John Robb
Coordinator, Unreached Peoples Task Force;
Chairman, Transformation Prayer Foundation.

I love the infectiousness of this book. It challenges us to higher levels of intimacy, of passion and of service. It is an uncompromising message of the power of the gospel. You will be left hungry for more of Jesus. As Gordon says, the more you look at Jesus, the more you are drawn to Him.

– Susan Partridge
Co-Founder/CEO, Live Free Foundation

This is a tremendous book! A timely book for our present age…a 'life manual' for the Christian who wants to be equipped for the fight of their lives. This journey, through the Cross will grip you more and more as you read. Many of the mysteries of the Gospel you have struggled with will be explained, as deeper mysteries are exposed. Gordon's book, which is also his life's journey, finishes with a crescendo like the cannon fire at the end of the Tchaikovsky's 1812 overture!

– Dr Jim Twelves
Christian Education: previous Head of teacher education, Alphacrucis College, Sydney, Australia

Movements begin with an idea, a vision, a burden. Our almighty God takes that small spark to create a blazing fire. Gordon ignites in the hearts of every reader a spark to join the work of God on earth today. Be prepared for the coming revival!

– Fouad Masri
President / CEO, Crescent Project

Every time Jesus sent anyone out to evangelize He told them all the same three things – but the primary command was to proclaim the Kingdom; yet most evangelism approaches ignore the Kingdom. Gordon's book proclaims the Kingdom of God! This is a comprehensive summary of what is needed today to reach the billions of souls that will come to Jesus in the next decades. We must embrace the way of the Cross, live a sacrificial life and obey God radically. The question remains, we will be part of this sacrificial army of people? I trust that this book will motivate you to say "Yes".

– Dr Barry Wissler
President, HarvestNet International

This urgent plea to release the power of the Cross brought me to tears several times. May it mess you up too!

– David Warnick
Author of "Is There More? Resurrecting Communion" Rathdrum, Idaho, USA

CONTENTS

MAKE GOD'S LOVE GO VIRAL!

Foreword   Brother Yun: "The viral Kingdom in China" 13
Introduction Confronted by God's Love 15

PART ONE: ACTIVATING GOD'S KINGDOM
Chapter 1: Making God's Love go viral! 25
Chapter 2: Creating a viral "Jesus culture" 31
Chapter 3: A pathway for Kingdom discipleship 39
Chapter 4: How David and Jesus modelled the Kingdom 45
Chapter 5: So how does this Kingdom operate? 51
Chapter 6: The heart of the matter 57
Chapter 7: It's fire we pray, it's fire we need 63

PART TWO: UNDERSTANDING CHRIST'S CROSS
Chapter 8   The foolishness of the Cross 73
Chapter 9   Two types of people and two laws 83
Chapter 10 The seven stages of the Cross 89
Chapter 11 Our slavery to the devil is broken 93
Chapter 12 Our intimacy with Father is restored 99
Chapter 13 Our inheritance is guaranteed 107
Chapter 14 Freed from my ego-self and "little old me" 111
Chapter 15 Spiritual lessons from marriage and baptism ... 119
Chapter 16 The final struggle of our self-life 127
Chapter 17 The daily walk of the Cross 133
Chapter 18 Shaking free of the "world system" 145

Chapter 19	The crossover point where many turn back	155
Chapter 20	Covenant: His last Will and Testament	163
Chapter 21	Our faith: the key to access intimacy	169
Chapter 22	Entering the Promised Land	179
Chapter 23	Transforming power of Sonship and Covenant	185
Chapter 24	Learning viral lifestyle by serving in His body	199
Chapter 25	The trigger of Sacrifice launches movements	215
Chapter 26	Some keys of the Kingdom	223
Chapter 27	Persecution and martyrdom cannot stop God	233
Appendix 1	Brother Yun on the Church in China	243
Appendix 2	Postscript by Pastor Surprise Sitole (Iris Ministry)	249

FOREWORD BY
BRO YUN, "THE HEAVENLY MAN"

THE VIRAL NATURE OF THE "KINGDOM"
A CHALLENGE FROM CHINA

In China, why is Christianity far more contagious and viral than it is in the West?

In this moment of history, just after the global pandemic of the Covid 19 virus spread from China to every Nation in the world, the challenge from heaven is "Pray for China!" The Lord Almighty says: "Not by might nor by power, but by my Spirit," (Zech 4:6). We need to believe in the power of the Holy Spirit to globally advance His viral Kingdom, which is far more powerful than any human virus! **I trust that this book will serve to activate God's Kingdom within you, through understanding the full power of Christ's Cross!**

I am a Chinese Christian, commonly called "The Heavenly Man", or Brother Yun. I love the teaching of the Apostle Paul so much. He says, 'I am not ashamed of the gospel, because it is the power of God for the salvation of everyone who believes: first for the Jew, then for the Gentile.' (Rom 1:16) In the last 50 years, the gospel of Jesus Christ has experienced an explosive revival in China. The population of believers has increased from 800,000 to over 100 million. We thank God, who heard our prayers; "the Lord added to our number daily, those who were being saved."

For this reason, I personally feel from the parable of the sower, that the church in China is the 4th type of soil, the good soil, which 'produces a crop, yielding a hundredfold.' (Matt 13:23) In the near future, China will not only be the country with the most Christians, she will also be the Nation that sends out the most missionaries. The Chinese House Churches survived simply through prayer, in a time of immense persecution, and in extreme difficulties. It is through prayer that the door of China slowly opened. The vision and mission of the millions of believers in the Chinese House Church movement is now to bring the Gospel "back to Jerusalem." Since the Gospel moved out westwards from Jerusalem, moving into Europe, then Africa, across to the Americas, and finally to the eastern seaboard of China, the Chinese Church have always believed it is their responsibility to carry the baton all the way back to where it began, moving with the Good News through the Buddhist, Hindu, and Muslim worlds which lie in between.

In these days, Jesus has raised up church leaders, who do not conform to the world's way of thinking. They are faithful and loyal to the end, praying day and night, spreading the gospel in secret, standing up for the truth, living for Jesus, and obeying Him. They have become the pillars that stand firm under persecution, accelerating the furtherance of the Kingdom of God. Even today God uses such leaders to protect his church.

Pray that the Holy Spirit will protect the church of China in this season, and that all the wonderful promises given, will be fulfilled. Let the "Heavenly Virus" spread like wild-fire. The Bible said: 'I AM coming soon. Hold on to what you have, so that no one will take your crown.' (Rev 3:11)

– "Heavenly Man"- Brother Yun
(See also Appendix 1: Bro Yun on the Church in China.)

INTRODUCTION

CONFRONTED BY GOD'S LOVE

With the backdrop of this foreword from Brother Yun, sharing about the viral nature of God's Kingdom across China, I have been passionately seeking for many years to know the power of the Cross to the extent that God's love can become contagious in my life. My reason for writing this book is that it took me years to understand God's love and the Cross, even though it is obviously the central focus of every Christian. I am indebted particularly to a man called Alan Vincent, who eventually became my father-in-law. He was first of all my spiritual father, and then it was through him that I slowly began to understand the incredible power and majesty of what Jesus did for us on the Cross, and how it released the power of God's Kingdom.

I have been seeking, searching, chasing, pursuing "something" for my entire spiritual life, since "it", or "He" burst in and confronted me 50 years ago, when I was trying to disprove its existence at Cambridge University. Jesus said, "seek first the Kingdom of God", which should have indicated to me that "it" or "He" was going to be elusive, hidden, and mysterious, but could be found through totally focussed, dedicated, passionate, and hungry pursuit. Over these years I've come to recognise that the "Kingdom", and the "Person", are one and the same - the man Christ Jesus. He has utterly consumed and transformed my life, and my life now radiates with the very person I have being pursuing!

As a young student at Cambridge, I had been confronted by the viral sweep of the Gospel through the University. I happened to be there for three years as a young Army Officer on an Army Scholarship, but I used the time and my subject of Social Psychology and Social Anthropology to dissect Christianity. I set about trying to disprove Religion, and then having met with real Christians who insisted that Christian faith was a relationship not a religion, I dared to try to prove that Jesus was a complete fraud and Christianity was a gigantic hoax.

The main reason why I hated God and Christians so much, was that I had become hooked up with an American cult at the age of 15, and for months I would get up at 4am every morning and study the Bible through their deceptive viewpoint. It took several years, but I was finally rescued by a wonderful Christian teacher, who slowly opened my eyes to their wrong theology. Deep down I must have been a "God seeker", as I remember then visiting Taizé monastery and even spent time at "La Pierre Qui Vire" a Benedictine monastery in the Morvan region of France. Every day I would just walk and read the Bible, desperately trying to make sense of it. It must have been the deep sense of disappointment in not finding answers, which created such a hatred of the Christian religion. It was with this background that I had joined the Army and finally took time out at Cambridge. (You can read all about my life story in the book "Harnessed for Adventure".)

In February 1974 however, 50 years ago now, the Kingdom of God burst forth in Cambridge: how and why, we may never know, but through the David Macinnes Mission, the Gospel swept virally through Cambridge. Many students came to faith including the famous "Nickys"- Gumbel, Lee, Wells, Campbell and Hills. Nicky Gumbel went on to develop the Alpha Course which has touched millions globally. Nicky and Sila Lee created the Marriage Course which also impacted millions. Other friends of theirs also came through in that mission, like Ken Costa, a leading financier in the

City of London and a core supporter of Alpha, and many current clergy and Bishops were born again during that 6-day Mission. I believe Nicky Hills was then one of the students who helped bring Justin Welby, the current Archbishop, to the Lord.

My stubborn aggression against the Mission finally culminated the day after it ended, with me spending a whole day writing out my summary of why the whole thing was a scam. That evening God himself graciously came into my room! (I was actually living on a houseboat, ironically moored in a place in Cambridge called "Jesus Lock") It's impossible to describe a visitation like that, but all I can say is that I cried uncontrollably on the floor, and that night I began my journey into faith. I had come into contact with the viral form of the Kingdom – Jesus himself!

Having married a daughter of missionaries to India, I was soon no stranger to missions. Rachel had spent most of her life in India, and then together we lived as missionaries in Africa and Asia in our early married life, watching the viral spread of the Gospel, when I was working as the Campaign Director for the Evangelist Reinhard Bonnke. On returning to UK, I had been pastoring a mission-minded church for many years, and I was also working for the Assemblies of God as their Missions Director for the Muslim World.

During this time back in the UK, I then watched the viral effect of a vision driven by the anointing of the Spirit; I saw it first-hand in my own town of Watford on our return from Africa and Asia: In the early 90's we had received a word from the Lord that He was going to birth something in Watford in youth ministry which would eclipse anything else happening in the country: arrogantly we thought God would do it in our church. However, I soon found myself face to face with a young youth pastor from a local Anglican Church with a bunch of 12 teenagers: he had a wild vision to start a youth movement in the Nation called Soul Survivor and he was asking us to help him.

I have to admit that as a Pentecostal I thought, "Can anything good come out of Nazareth (the Anglican Church)!" Fortunately however, we swallowed our pride and this group of 12 began to meet in our church lounge, writing songs and worshipping and then during the summer they started their first summer gathering using our Church Hall. All we could do was pray for them and bless them. It wasn't long before they were gathering 1000 young people locally and for many years they were drawing over 30,000 young people to their Summer Camps. We are well aware of the later leadership failings, but during those years, youth ministry and also worship ministry was radically and virally changed by Soul Survivor, and the host of anointed worship leaders beginning with Matt Redman.

In the year 2000 I began to work with Brother Yun, commonly called the "Heavenly Man" after his book about his miraculous experiences of revival and persecution in China. Together we set up the "Back to Jerusalem Foundation" in UK, to begin to spread the news of the rapid growth of the Chinese Church, and their commitment over the coming years to train and send out 100,000 Chinese missionaries to bring the Gospel through the Muslim, Hindu and Buddhist nations – all the way back to the source of the Gospel in Jerusalem. Their understanding is simply that the Gospel travelled westwards from Jerusalem until it finally reached China, and they feel now that they have taken the baton and are running fast to complete the task of bringing it back to the city of Jerusalem where it all began!

I guess I considered myself a passionate, radical, "on-fire" type of Christian....that is until I began to work and travel with Brother Yun! I very quickly became aware that my understanding of the Kingdom was far short of not only his understanding, but also of his experience: he had experienced a type of viral Christianity which I could hardly get my head around. He would speak of the wild-fire revival that was sweeping through China from the 1980's onwards. The Kingdom I was used to, considered sacrifice and laying down your life for the Gospel as its highest form of service; but with Brother Yun, being willing to lay your life down and be martyred for the Gospel was just their entry point into Kingdom service - Discipleship 101!

In those early years of working together, God was on my case: my whole Christian worldview and even my Christian values were being confronted with what I came to call "the Heavenly Virus" - after the "Heavenly Man". I had seen the remarkable moves of God in all our campaigns with Reinhard Bonnke; I had witnessed tens of thousands of people being swept into the Kingdom of God in each meeting, together with remarkable miracles of healing and deliverance....and yet, this was something else.

Remember that Jesus burst onto the scene proclaiming: "something greater is here!" - far greater than the most magnificent building like the Temple, far greater than the wealth and wisdom of Solomon, and even far greater than the powerful ministry of Jonah whose ministry brought a whole city to God! The "Kingdom" arrived with Jesus and this contagious and highly infectious "heavenly virus" was now living and active in Him. Wherever he went, there was an outbreak of the Kingdom. It was uncontainable, irrepressible, and unstoppable.

It was this irrepressible, unstoppable Kingdom that confronted me years later in my comfortable western form of Christianity, which seemed to have lost its contagion, and which certainly couldn't be described as viral. On returning from the mission field in 1990, we took over the Senior Leadership of a network of four excellent Churches in four towns. We tried every evangelistic scheme to bring revival to that area of West Herts. We put up a 1000-seater tent in one of the cities and preached for 2 weeks, and then a 2000-seater in another town, and then hired the Football Stadium for another town; we even brought in Evangelist Reinhard Bonnke; we put leaflets through every door...we saturated that area with evangelistic activity. Yes, we did see several hundred people coming to Christ, but where was the "something greater"? Where was that "Heavenly virus" of the Kingdom that caused multiplication, not just addition.

I remember becoming increasingly desperate to see the Kingdom come. Even though our Churches were the success story of the area, as their Senior Pastor I knew deep down that this wasn't an outbreak of the "Kingdom". I began to go on "walk about" – not telling my Church! - but I began to visit anything or anyone where I heard that there had been a significant outbreak of God. After 3 months, this search led me to a small church plant where there were only about 50 people, and the worship was dire: but when the visiting speaker arrived, I sensed in my spirit that "something greater is here"!

I couldn't wait to run down to the front and ask him to pray for me, but as I arrived at the front I was hit by what I can only describe as a lightning bolt of a million volts! I am a quiet public school, ex-Army Officer type, but when God just kept on turning up the voltage, I thought I was going to die: I screamed and screamed for God not to kill me. He didn't listen, and for the next 45 minutes I was "fried" alive by the fire of God. It was both a significant time of breaking something off me, as well as imparting "something greater" within me.

That experience introduced me to the reality of the fire of God: I was too weak to walk to the car afterwards and my friends just bundled me into the car to drive me home. Suddenly it was as if heaven opened up a vast technicolour screen, for just a second, and I watched the vision in amazement as the fire of God swept through whole Muslim nations, with Jesus being unveiled to millions of Muslims!

I imagined how Abraham must have felt, as God showed him the countless millions of his future descendants: like Abraham, in that single fleeting moment of vision, I too became a believer, with unshakeable faith in God's passion for Muslim people, and his plan to unveil Jesus to them and to bring them into his Kingdom.

It was that encounter with the fire of God and the subsequent vision that changed the course of my life. I found that I was now compelled by the Spirit, and under His orders: I was still active as a Senior Pastor, but more and more I was being drawn into that area of ministry amongst Muslims. A chance meeting of a converted Muslim radical, led to a bond of friendship, and the formation in 1997 of the Bible Channel on satellite TV, a Church without boundaries with hundreds of programmes being created in Arabic and later in Urdu, seeking to birth house churches in people's homes across the Muslim world. I was beginning to notice the viral aspect of the Gospel.

It was this Kingdom which led us as a couple to leave all our ministries behind in 2005 and obey God's direction for me (an Assemblies of God Pentecostal minister) to become an Anglican Vicar in the heart of Oxford! We closed down my wife's ministry of Heartcry, and the London Prayernet, and all my work with the Assemblies of God, and we moved to Oxford, where I became Parish Vicar in St Aldates Church. The following year through a friendship with a missionary called Tim Green, we birthed a prayer movement called Mahabba ("Love" in Arabic) which began to train and equip ordinary Christians to unveil Jesus to Muslim people.

In its early days, this became a viral movement, with Mahabba networks spreading across the country, and even further into Europe, and other Nations. The vision of millions of Muslims being swept into the Kingdom of God still burns in my soul, but on a visit to the Outpouring in Cwmbran, God confronted my unbelief again: the same fire of God fell on me, and I was thrown to the floor; for what seemed like an hour or more, I felt God wrestling with me, throwing me from side to side. All I could hear throughout that time was the Holy Spirit challenging me: "Why will you not surrender and believe me for 30 million Muslims?" I'm ashamed to say that it took over an hour for me to surrender my unbelief and only then the fire lifted. I was then able to stand, knowing that faith for 30 million Muslims had been injected into me! It is impossible to describe such moments, when seeds of faith are implanted in your soul.

I have shared all these personal experiences in this introduction, so that you can see the pattern of God's challenges throughout my life. I hear the heart cry of Jesus still echoing in my soul: "I've come to start a fire on this earth - how I wish it were blazing right now! I've come to change everything, turn everything right side up - how I long for it to be finished! Do you think I came to smooth things over and make everything nice? Not so. I've come to disrupt and confront!" (Message: Luke 12:49).

In this book we explore this viral Kingdom, and how everything essentially is centered on fully understanding the Cross of Christ: this book will take you on a journey through the seven stages of the Cross which is designed to activate God's "heavenly virus" within you. Our cry is "let's make God's love go viral!"

PART ONE

1

ACTIVATING GOD'S KINGDOM

CHAPTER 1

MAKING GOD'S LOVE GO VIRAL

On Pentecost morning God woke me up with this poem. It just poured out onto paper and I felt such a strong sense that this was a prophetic word from God for this generation:

The Heavenly Virus - God's response to Corona Virus

In 2020 Covid Virus hit the nations of the world
But strangely this was also when God's global plan unfurled,
Raising leaders in the church who saw with perfect vision
To impart faith and hope and reconcile division

Those were the days of lockdown which stopped us in our tracks
When our old wineskins failed, revealing all the cracks;
We saw so clearly then that it's "not by might or power"
But "by God's Holy Spirit" who is needed in this hour

As in those days of old - there in Jerusalem
With those disciples locked down in that upper room,
It seemed to all the world that day that Rome had clearly won,
But little did they know right then, that God had just begun!

As those nails pierced his hands, and that spear pierced his side,
The world grew dark and grey, every hope and dream just died;
There on that Cross at Calvary, the devil's fury was outpoured,
But God reached down and seized that Cross, and it became his sword!

There it was that God himself, made a spectacle and stripped
The devil of his power and saw all his demons whipped!

That moment could have easily brought a global wide disaster
But here is where our Lord became our King and sovereign Master

So today when it once seemed this virus might have won
We all now need to come to faith that our God has just begun!
Old ways, traditions, wineskins, – all of these have stopped
And God has pruned his church, and all religion has been cropped

Now it is our God's turn – to send his "heavenly virus!"-
A global wide awakening, a revival flow amongst us
Gone are all the man-made hierarchies and structures
Things that make us sterile, with fear, control and ruptures

This is the day we need to seize - God's church must be a "movement"-
Every believer now empowered to know we're "heaven-sent",
Discipled by servant leaders who know how to equip
An army of believers – each one held "in his grip!"

Like those lepers in lockdown, back in Elisha's day
We all will soon discover that the enemy must pay!
Every crippling constriction, every limit now has gone
Our enemies have fled away, in terror and abandon

Now we're walking out, to a totally new landscape
Millions once captive, are seeking all ways to escape.
These years of this cruel virus showed the people they can't cope-
Now they're yearning deep inside for our messages of hope.

God has shaken, and He's shaken – just His realm now remains.
Gone are the excuses, the deceptions and the games.
People are just crying for relationship and touch -
God's signal to us all, who've been given so, so much!

So come on all you leaders, let's arise and let us shine!
Let's make God's love go viral! Come on! Now it's our time!
Let's rise up with his weapons of unity and prayer;
Let's demonstrate with grace to all - that we care - and yes, we dare!

In this first chapter, I want to look at the whole process of "making God's Love go viral." As we look at this process, we have to face the pivotal key in discipling people into the Kingdom: it is this simple truth that "you become like the person you bond with." If you bond with someone, there will be an automatic transfer of life and values from that person. The reverse is also true: if there is no bond, there is no transfer of life and values.

I need to interject here to explain that of course there is also great value in the academic transfer of knowledge through bible schools, courses, and classes. Knowledge has to be passed on, but if this is the only means of the transfer of knowledge and values, then the very core of the Gospel is not imparted: this is a "life to life" impartation. Jesus lived, ate, and slept alongside his disciples. Thousands heard his words, but the disciples had a direct daily impartation of life from Jesus. This transformed them into powerful apostles.

They were all misfits and people whom we would hardly have chosen to lead us; but His direct personal time with them changed their lives. God could have sent a remote booming sound from heaven and tried to impart this indirectly: in some ways this is the story of the Old Testament which obviously didn't work. So instead He chose to give us His own Son in human form, so there could be not only a "sound" but also a "touch" – they could hear Jesus, but they could also feel Jesus, and personally interact with him. This bond enabled the life transfer from heaven to earth. Any parent will know this is true: your words alone have no power to change your kids!

So, what does this have to do with "making God's love go viral"? Let me explain how this began. The disciples are gathered in the upper room for an intimate meal with Jesus: towards the end of the meal, He breaks bread and begins to outline to them that this is actually a covenant meal – He is passing over to them everything He is and everything He stands for – He is putting it into their hands. He says "guys, tonight I'm giving you the Kingdom! I am putting my whole life's work and ministry into your hands. All that I have is yours, and all that I am, I am imparting it to you!" They are touched but mystified and nothing happens immediately. Within a matter of weeks however, this time bomb explodes. By then, He has wrestled with demonic powers on the Cross, and then stripped the devil of all his power and authority and risen back from the dead - not just coming back to life, but returning as "the man from Heaven", not subject anymore to the powers of sin, sickness, and death.

He bursts onto the scene as a "new creation". He's walking through walls, and just appearing from nowhere. I'm trying to help you to capture what the disciples are experiencing: they are witnessing a hell-defeating, death-defying, transcendent spiritual being who passionately loves and cares for them; and then He pours this spiritual power and love into them and all over them. What a life changing moment! Now this was the moment God's love went viral!

As I began wrestling with God as a Church leader, desperate to see the Kingdom of God break through, I knew it had to have something to do with the fire of God. As a network of four churches, we were probably the most successful church network in the area, but in my spirit, I wasn't satisfied. "Come on God! Where is the Kingdom power and authority? Where is the fire?" Without telling the churches what I was doing, I began to look everywhere for signs of a Kingdom breakthrough and secretly started visiting all kinds of churches - I referred briefly to this in the introduction. About three months later I was depressed from finding no visible sign of real Kingdom power, but then I heard of something happening which was unexplainable. It was about an hour away, so I drove down there with two friends.

There was nothing special about the service but when the visiting speaker stood up to speak, I was rivetted! The Kingdom, the fire - it was all there! I ran up to the front as he finished speaking, but before I could reach him, I was literally thrown to the floor by the Holy Spirit. I began to feel fire pouring through me. It became stronger and stronger, until it felt like a million volts. I was screaming for God not to kill me, as it was so painful. Suddenly my eyes were open to a gripping open vision of the fire of God pouring through Nation after Nation, many of which were the Islamic strongholds.

A week later, I was trying to explain all this to my church when suddenly to my amazement, people began to fall off their chairs at the back of the hall and lay on the floor laughing or crying. God's love was going viral! It was an unstoppable force. I had seen this in my earlier life in Africa as a Campaign Director for an evangelist called Reinhard Bonnke. At times the Spirit of God would fall on vast crowds and they would be laughing or crying and often whole sections would fall to the ground. This goes beyond our theology and reasoning, but it confirms that God will be God: He will not be put in a box and contained. When Jesus tells us to pray "Let Your Kingdom come", He's thinking of moments like this when God's Kingdom sovereignly breaks into our world.

It was the same in China. While I worked with one of the Chinese underground church pastors called Brother Yun, or the "heavenly man", he would speak with pain of those early days in the 1950's when Mao Tsedong closed every church, burnt every Bible and placed all the pastors in labour camps – the Church of China died overnight. Yun would then light up and tell us of the viral wave of the Holy Spirit who was still there in China – the Government had no way of removing Him: thousands were being touched sovereignly by God, with people meeting in caves and forests, weeping their hearts out to prepare a "highway" for the Spirit of God to come in power. The love of God went viral carried largely by young people in their late teens and early twenties. Many of the male leaders were imprisoned, so 70% of the viral leaders were young women who were so anointed to carry God's love and gossip the Gospel throughout China.

These were the hidden force of evangelists and church planters who were carrying the fire of this Kingdom leadership. Under the anointing, "in Christ", there is no such thing as "male or female", so our church practice and theology need to bow to God's superior wisdom. This was the David-heart of those "laid-down life" band of warriors who sacrificially took the Gospel to every corner of China – often risking their own lives. This should inspire us that we too can "make God's love go viral" in our world and our culture.

CHAPTER 2

CREATING A VIRAL "JESUS CULTURE"

The Apostles, imitating Jesus Christ himself, created a culture which became the viral "Jesus culture" which swept through the known world. Jesus served us sacrificially in His last-ditch assault on the kingdom of darkness: as he laid His life down on the Cross, giving up his life for us and dying instead of us, he took ultimate responsibility for all our sins. My Bible says that it was that one act which totally disarmed the enemy of our souls, and as a result He also conquered death, and gave us the right to be eternally joined to him in unending Life! This book is about the Cross and the viral Kingdom that it introduced to humanity. May we be inspired to follow Him into some of life's greatest adventures to seek and save the lost and may this inspire us to rescue millions of people from the devil's grip.

Having spent many years as a British Army Officer, my greatest inspiration growing up as a Christian was a soldier, the young soldier David, who not only took out Goliath, but also inspired a whole generation of misfits, and ruffians; when King Saul saw the way this youthful shepherd-turned-soldier won the hearts of his people, there was an immediate clash of kingdoms: the "head and shoulders above" culture of life, with all its top-down management and control, was no match against the simplicity of David's culture of a "life laid down to serve his men". Saul was the professional, but totally unanointed. David in contrast, was the servant-hearted, but truly anointed man of God. His was a life laid down for Kingdom purpose - to influence, mentor, and release his men into their destiny.

Many of the people around us are like the men who gathered around David out there in the wilderness in the cave of Adullam, when he was running from Saul: like them, many are distressed in their situations, discontented with life and severely in debt. They are looking for an authentic life to follow. Often instead, they are presented with a group of professional "religious experts" who may well know all their theology, but who lack the sheer simplicity of someone who has a profound intimacy with God and is capable of reflecting Him and speaking for Him under the anointing of the Holy Spirit.

We see from this that Kingdom culture is completely upside down to the culture which is offered to the church from the religious, business and management fields. Those have their value and may look good externally, with all their structures and sense of growing empire, but they fail to catch the pure viral magic of the close-knit relationships which turned David's motley crew into one of the most effective fighting forces of the day. These "mighty men" were soon to establish the Kingdom across a vast region, which was to last for a generation. Sadly, many churches choose to implement the more structural "empire" model, which looks great from the outside, but they miss the grass roots viral relational model which is true Kingdom. Now, this has nothing to do with size, as I know some massive Kingdom churches: it has everything to do with what is hidden in our hearts, generating this viral movement.

In its simplest form, Kingdom culture is about *a life laid down sacrificially, which gives us the ability to impact, influence, and infect others with the living culture or heavenly Kingdom "virus" that we are carrying through the power of the Spirit.* Some of the cultural characteristics you'll find burning in their hearts are core values like these:

» **presence:** the way they value and carry His presence

» **purity:** their commitment to holiness – single-minded with no distractions.

- » **purpose:** their divine sense of purpose
- » **passion:** their passion for God, for people and for reaching souls for Christ
- » **perseverance:** their ability to persevere through trials
- » **power:** their anointing to move with the power of God
- » **peace:** their commitment to reconciliation – people are never their enemy!

Very often you will find in them that there is also a hidden life with God, which accounts for the fact that all the above are undergirded and sustained by three life-values and qualities:

- » **prayer:** their disciplined regular times of intimate prayer
- » **praise:** their decision to praise God in everything – especially tough times!
- » **prophecy:** their bold decision to declare God's word until situations change – the essence of prophecy

These core values are part of the engine room which generates all of the other values. They create, as it were, an inner "fire in our bones" which others can identify within us: but it is wild and uncontrollable, just like natural fire. Jeremiah cried out that he just couldn't hold it in, he just had to release the fire that was in him. It is this "Holy Spirit and fire anointing" which can run wild through a whole generation and a whole people group.

This culture is simply infecting the generation around us with the "Jesus culture" we are carrying. We see in the letter to the Ephesians which was written as a training manual for a Church in spiritual warfare, that Jesus didn't send anyone else to do the job – He came Himself. He came to personally infect us with the Kingdom culture of "peace" (irene) that He was carrying. This word "irene" signifies "restored covenant" after a broken relationship, to the extent that the two opposing parties become one; secondly it signifies a "broken bone fused together" where the break is now stronger than the surrounding bone.

Jesus, our Warrior King, came carrying this extraordinary viral quality of "peace" so that he could set us free from all the hopelessness, bondage, brokenness, and division of the enemy. He came to be bonded with us, using God's covenant as His mechanism of bonding us to Himself and to each other. In Him we are all "fused together" – a bit like "mashed potatoes" once all the skins are removed. We are no longer thick-skinned, independent, with all our facades, shields, and protective mechanisms. We become transparent with each other – living "in the light"- which enables the Holy Spirit to touch, heal and restore, all those broken places in our lives.

This is the place where God comes to re-infect us with His "culture", which is His Glory! He is our "Glory and the lifter of our head." The early church was so united and so contagious – for just this reason: it is what I call a "heavenly virus!" Sadly, the devil immediately countered with "religion", which slowly killed the viral quality of the sacrificial Jesus relationships. The devil sowed such division and fear into the church, that the glory departed, and religion reigned with just a few small flashes of revival outbreaks. We see here that religion is totally opposite to a Kingdom lifestyle and discipleship.

It may help just to pause here for a moment and take stock of what God's eternal dream was as a Father, when he birthed us in Genesis: His Kingdom dream was always to create passionately close and restored intimacy with us His children – to walk and talk intimately with us, with nothing hidden and everything laid bare – as it were, "naked but unashamed". We were created in his very image, born to reflect the very character and nature of Father God. The Bible calls this "outshining" characteristic of God "His Glory" and this is quite simply the radiance, reflection and "outshining" of the perfect harmony, love and peace of the Godhead – a reflection of relational intimacy and unity at its utter perfection!

Peter really had a revelation of this and called this state of intimate unity of life and purpose a state of "koinonia" – which we weakly translate "fellowship". This is the state of life that we are beckoned into, with the one proviso that we must "come clean": the whole concept of "living in the light" denotes a decision to hide nothing and be utterly honest and transparent, with every veil and facade removed.

Can you see now, why Paul says that we can all then stand together and draw close to Him with "unveiled faces", like polished mirrors reflecting the very Glory of God, being transformed continuously with an ever-increasing Glory on each of us? All this is the work the Holy Spirit loves to pour into us – which is why this is "target number one" on the enemy hitlist. He will do anything to smash that mirror of intimacy and unity, and make us hide from each other in guilt, fear and shame.

Kingdom is about creating a viral culture in people which is unstoppable. It can't be learnt just from books, so it has to be experienced and received from another Kingdom believer through an impartation by the Holy Spirit. As with God, it is simply a reflection or "outshining" of who we are - it is our very nature. Too many people are deceived into putting their whole effort and focus on the external wineskin of education, vision, mission, church structures, programmes, and processes.

The extraordinary thing about creating a viral "culture" reflecting the very heart of who we are, is that mysteriously a fresh flexible "wineskin" just forms naturally as the whole focus is on the wine of His presence, and the peace and joy of the unity of spirit amongst us. So, when new people come into contact with us, the first thing that impacts and influences them is the infectious culture that we have created amongst us. Children naturally take on the "home culture" that their parents have created, and it's the same with God's children. This Kingdom culture is far more "caught" than just "taught!"

What is at stake here is our deeply held value system: what we value highly will naturally be imparted to others. This will shape what we see and what we speak, and eventually it becomes our own culture. However, this whole process takes time. Instant culture is a myth. Jesus said an interesting thing: that what we truly value will burn right at the centre of our heart and being, and this in turn will shape the very things we speak. We begin to speak and live our values, and they become infectious to others.

Kingdom people define what is valuable to them by constantly emphasizing and personally doing what they value. If they do something, their followers will do it. If they don't personally do something, their followers won't. This is the same law as parenting, because disciples learn clear values as they copy and imitate people living out the Kingdom. Paul told his followers to imitate him as he was imitating Christ. These disciples are not looking for another course, but rather they are looking for a life to follow and reproduce.

Let's return then to our young soldier David and look more closely at how he grew into such a remarkable man of the Kingdom who was able to reflect the heart of God. At the core of David's heart and life burned one simple thing: his revelation of his unshakeable covenant with Almighty God. He learnt this when he was protecting his sheep from the lion and the bear. It is often in a time of crisis and desperation that "the penny drops", and we receive a clear revelation that God is for us and not against us, utterly faithful and true to His promises. This connects us to Father God in a totally different way, because it is in these times that we discover who we are in God, and who He is on the inside of us!

I describe this process of transformation like this: **desperation** leads us into a fresh **revelation** of God and of ourselves; this revelation then leads us into a deeper **consecration** of our lives to Him; this in turn leads us into a life **transformation**, which causes us to focus our life work on the **proclamation**, **demonstration** and

manifestation of the Spirit of God within us. That's quite a mouthful! But at the heart of all this is the simple revelation of the law of covenant: its all of Him for all of me – it's all or nothing.

His death becomes my death – the death of the "little me" inside which has dominated my life. Then His resurrection life is imparted to me and, in this divine exchange, I go from "minus to plus" letting go of all the negatives that ruled me in order to be clothed with His glory and power. In that same moment, we receive His mantle of anointing, His weapons of warfare, His authority over demonic powers, His name, His Spirit, His promises, and His love and power. Wow! What an exchange! This is the "Jesus Kingdom culture" burning on the inside of us which becomes infectious and viral to all we engage with.

CHAPTER 3

A PATHWAY FOR KINGDOM DISCIPLESHIP

As a house group leader in my earlier years, I had seen the simplicity of this relational Kingdom, and had identified five simple steps to train people into this Kingdom. This training is not confined to books and methods: as I said earlier, "it is more caught than taught!" The first step is to find a bunch of hungry, desperate people, who really want God. Often it will be people who are in pain in some area of their life We are surrounded by them daily, as people today are looking for a spiritual encounter, though they may not be interested in church or religion.

Remember our young soldier David who chose the debtors, distressed, and discontented (1 Sam 22). Then look at Jesus in his choice of disciples, and the apostle's choice too - "the sexually immoral, idolaters, adulterers, homosexuals, thieves, greedy, drunkards, slanderers, and swindlers"- this list of disciples in 1 Cor 6:9 might send shivers through some pastors! These early disciples were all misfits, but hungry and desperate for God. What we are talking about is the ability to look for those "treasures in darkness" who are not obvious to the religious eye. We need those "Kingdom eyes" like Michelangelo, who just kept hammering away at blocks of stone to release the "angels" that he could see trapped inside. Our streets are full of such people, if we could just see them with those "Kingdom eyes". It is tempting for Churches to look for "nice" people to fill the pews, and so sadly these Churches may never witness the life transforming power of the Cross.

Secondly, and probably the most costly, is that we have to give ourselves relationally to these imperfect people. Just six months after we married, we were asked to lead a connect group, as well as being closely involved with shaping the church youth group. Our house group consisted of five young people who had just come out of a cult, three young men who were struggling with their sexual identity and life's purpose, a returned missionary who felt a failure and others, who along with us, were also complex! However, the common factor was that we were all hungry for God and desperate! God told us just to give ourselves unconditionally to these people and so we broke bread every time we met and prayed for each other. The group doubled in six months: our friends from the cult were baptized in the Spirit and two of them later became leaders of significant churches. Those who had battled with their sexual identity fell in love, got married and had kids, another set up a national ministry to help young men with their sexuality; the ex-missionary set up the most effective charity to reach the homeless and addicted in our town. Something was obviously imparted and transferred as we bonded together as a group!

The third step, and probably the most misunderstood, is that we need to help each one of them to have a revelation of the Cross. (this is why this book has been written) This is a journey however, and when Jesus walked with his disciples, he slowly led them from their early shallow understanding of commitment, through to "if you want to follow me, you need to take up your Cross daily!" Only this revelation of the Cross in our lives will set us free from the core thing inside us which is crippling our lives - our own ego, and the "little me" which so often rules and dominates and controls our lives. The Cross was not only meant for Jesus; it was meant also to crucify the "little me" - my ego - so that I could be free from this wicked internal slavery to my own ego and self-centred independence. That's why Paul says to the Corinthians who were plagued with all kinds of problems, that his central message and solution for them was the Cross. He just preached "Christ crucified": read on!

We must be very careful in our self-focussed "pamper me" culture, that our counselling doesn't pamper the "little me" inside people who are hurting, posturing them as victims of difficult and painful situations: that route may never lead to freedom. Yes, they do need our love and compassion, but they personally need to bring themselves – that self-centred "little me" - to the Cross and get delivered from themselves. Jesus didn't come to just improve our lifestyle: he came to help us remove the "little me" from the picture. Paul almost shouts out in Galatians 2:20: "Hey, guys, it's worked! I really have been delivered from that crippling "little me". I have been crucified with Christ and this thing doesn't live inside me and terrorize me anymore. I'm now free to live a life of faith, trusting the precious Son of God who loved me so much that he died for me and enabled me also to die to myself."

The fourth step is a natural follow-on to this third step, although it takes time, faith, and patience. We are now in a position to infect them with the viral qualities of Kingdom values which we personally carry. As we said earlier, every Kingdom principle is "upside down" to natural worldly principles. So here we see in the natural that a virus dies as soon as its host is dead; but in the Kingdom, it is the opposite: as soon as we become dead to ourselves, we become perfect carriers of the "heavenly virus" of the Kingdom. These core values which burn in our souls such as valuing God's presence, purity, purpose, passion, perseverance, power, and peace, begin to influence and impact the lives of our disciples. As they grow closer to us they are then further influenced by those hidden qualities of our prayer life, our commitment to praise, and prophesy into every situation.

In Mark 3:14 we see that Jesus simply chose 12 people, who to us might look somewhat dysfunctional; He chose these people "to be with him" so that they could be infected with His quality of life, His humility and obedience, His respect for the anointing of the Holy Spirit, His servanthood, His transparency and vulnerability, His commitment and faith in His covenant. Whatever we do and whatever we value will be imparted naturally to those whom we come alongside relationally. One thing I have learnt however is that the primary quality I look for in potential carriers of the Kingdom, is their "loyalty and faithfulness". Why is this so important? All they need is "loyalty and faithfulness" so that they can bond with you, and the other values are transferred naturally as your culture infects them. Be very careful however, never to abuse such loyalty and faithfulness: this can sometimes be the grounds for a bullying and controlling culture to develop where leaders are insecure.

Finally, step number five is having the faith and courage to send these disciples out in the power of the Holy Spirit to infect other people. Jesus chose His twelve disciples just "to be with Him and then to send them out in the power of the Holy Spirit; and then he gave them His authority to heal the sick and cast out demons." (Mark 3:14-15) Jesus's top priority was to spend 3 years with 12 men! Day and night, he was with them, imparting His Kingdom values into their lives. This is why there was such a rapid spread of this viral Kingdom culture: they made God's love go viral!

Before you jump on the bandwagon and shout "Hey! I'm all in!" we do all need to check our motivation. What we are not talking about here is training people to help us in our ministry. If you sign up to this, your heart motivation must be to train other broken hungry desperate people so that you can release their potential and their destiny – not just yours! The heart of the Kingdom is the heart of a servant, serving others "to make others look good". Like Paul with the Colossians, we want to "present *them* perfect in Christ" (Col 1:28-29), and as he writes to the Galatians, he is "in travail in prayer and intercession until Christ is formed in *them*" (Gal 4:19)

The bottom line in all of this, is the way we perceive people. We tend so often to judge people by externals: young David would have been missed! The most critical factor is to ask the Holy Spirit to retrain us to see people's hearts, not their externals. Sometimes the "worst are the best" as they are people of influence and drive – yes, maybe harnessed by the wrong spirit, but certainly perfect in God's hands to form apostles, prophets, pastors, teachers and evangelists.

Can you see the future apostle in the aggressive Iman shouting out his terrorist rhetoric? Can you see the future prophet in the high-profile witch or warlock, or the pastors in the couple who are desperately struggling through a divorce? I could go on, but it is essential that we ask God for these "Kingdom eyes" which can see people as God sees them.

Beware of allowing any area of your own personal insecurity to cloud your dealings with people. Beware! It often leads to bullying, control, crushing and abuse: in the end, your disciples must have the potential of becoming your friends, and going far further than you in the Kingdom. That's what we expect of natural children! Like any parent/child relationship, there are often high limitations and boundaries to begin with, but this slowly reduces as the child grows in self-discipline and self-awareness.

Modelling this steady release, follows the way Jesus began to send out his disciples to do the simple things like healing the sick and raising the dead! Yes, we still have the right to challenge them into their destiny, but we constantly encourage, affirm and release them like arrows. In a relational Kingdom, this often means minimal control, but high friendship and accountability.

Finally, let me end this chapter with the mystery of what happens when you give your confidence to people, and empower them. In the spirit realm, you are actually giving them something tangible:

they will suddenly discover that they can do impossible things! When Jesus breathes on his disciples and sends them out, He empowers them and gives them His authority. He expects them to go out and do everything He has been doing, in terms of healing the sick, raising the dead and casting out demons.

If you give people a job they can do, they will probably go out and do it in their own strength and gifting. Instead, throw them in the deep end and ask them to do a humanly impossible job, and you will launch them out into the deep where they will have to utterly depend on the Holy Spirit. They will either sink or swim: so be ready to fish them out of their failures but then graciously encourage them back into it again and again. We do this with toddlers all the time, picking them up and encouraging them to walk until one day they are off! One day your disciples will be off over the horizon - launched into the Kingdom, depending entirely on the anointing of the Holy Spirit!

CHAPTER 4
HOW DAVID AND JESUS MODELLED IT

We've looked at the young soldier David, and we've seen how his laid-down servant heart mobilized and shaped a generation. Let's compare David's model of Kingdom life with Jesus's model and let's see what we can learn through comparing them.

Firstly, they both started training their disciples and growing a group culture out in the desert rather than in the city where there were so many distractions. They both chose a band of what we would today call "nobodies", and then they decided to commit themselves to simply living with them for a significant period of time. These misfits and outcasts developed a strong relational bonding with both David and Jesus, to the extent that the men were able to watch their leaders close at hand and personal - nothing hidden. They watched the integrity of their life and slowly trust was formed, then commitment, and finally a willingness to serve and obey. With David's men, there is that touching moment of total surrender, when they shouted out "We are yours! Success to you and those who help you! God is on your side." (I Chron 12-18)

Both David and Jesus then divide their men into smaller groups so that in turn the men can be more intimate and transparent and trusting with each other. Finally, when they began to see that the men were ready, they then commissioned them and released them to go in pairs and share the same values and culture with anyone they met. They both released an authority to their men, although Jesus went one step further and actually empowered them to do what He'd been doing in terms of the miraculous healing and deliverance from demons. We don't know how long David stayed with his men, but Jesus was with them day and night for three years!

As I said in the last chapter, both David and Jesus discovered that a mystery took place when they gave their confidence to their men and released them to do impossible things. The motley crew of "nobodies" became David's "mighty men" and Jesus's "apostles". What I find so moving is recognizing the moment when they both knew without a doubt that they had succeeded in transforming the lives of these men. It was at the moment that they both cried out the same thing: "I am thirsty!"

Both were thirsty, but Jesus's thirst was spiritual – a desperate thirst for the souls of men and women globally. We see first with David that his cry was met by his men showing their willingness to risk losing their lives to venture behind enemy lines just to fetch water so that David could drink and be satisfied. Remarkably similar, the cry of Jesus has echoed down the centuries, evoking the same selfless sacrifice from countless warriors of the faith, who have ventured "behind enemy lines" to rescue souls to satisfy the heart of God. Many have paid the ultimate sacrifice and have actually laid down their lives, which in turn has precipitated a wave of fresh revival: as Tertullian said: "the blood of the martyrs is the seed of the Church".

Let's also compare the pathway that both David and Jesus chose in their growth into Kingdom culture. David started in the wilderness with his men, but by the time he managed to establish his base in Hebron they were bonded to him. Hebron means "the place of close association, or fellowship". Jesus similarly started with his men out in the wilderness, and by the time they reached the upper room, they were all bonded together with him.

This is where the Kingdom is counter intuitive: everything in the natural screams "You've made it! They are all yours, and you have such amazing unity and fellowship!" It is so tempting for us to stay in this "happy-clappy" place of close fellowship, basking in our success. Kingdom however is upside down and demands a humanly senseless decision to risk everything.

Staying in Hebron, the place of fellowship, was never going to allow the Kingdom to go viral, because the highest place of Zion was still occupied by all the "ites" which had never been removed. David risked his life sneaking up the water shaft at night and took the whole of Zion by surprise. I have followed his steps up that water shaft, and it was a deeply spiritual experience as I told Father once again that I never want to shy away from being willing to lay my life down. Many who similarly work amongst Muslim people have had to make this decision.

Jesus in the same way could have rested in the upper room with an immense sense of fulfillment, with John lying closely beside Him and all the rest of the disciples totally bonded with Him – all except one man, Judas. Jesus was tempted to pull back from going to Zion, the place of the Cross, and it must have been a massive spiritual battle as He knew this was going to cost him everything. We see his anguish in John 12 when he groans "My soul is in absolute turmoil, but how am I going to respond to this? Am I going to ask Father to rescue me from this agonizing death. No way! This is the very reason I came to this moment! Come on Father, let's glorify your Name!"

This one decision enabled God's plan to go ahead and it was on the Cross that the Kingdom of God totally disarmed and destroyed the devil's kingdom. Let's just pause for a moment and reflect on whether we personally have compromised and drawn back at that vital moment of decision: "Lord, let your will be done, whatever the cost to my life! Let your Kingdom come!"

Having seen how similar the Kingdom pathways are for both David and Jesus, let's look at the process God uses throughout the Bible to mature the embryo seed of Kingdom life. There are no short cuts in developing character, skills or muscles: it is hard graft!

Hardship, massive opposition, and major delays are what we meet along this pathway, however at every moment there is Grace and a fresh potential to get more and more revelation of how God's Kingdom works.

Firstly God says in Hebrews 12, "Come on, endure these times of *hardship* as discipline, because I'm only going to take this seriously and discipline you because I love you and because you are part of the family. Through this time of hardship, you're going to really grow in character and perseverance, and you'll find yourself becoming more and more like me, with a deep growing sense of inner confidence and peace."

Secondly God allows you to go through *massive opposition* and you will discover that every wild opponent pops their head above the parapet and goes for you – often not from non-believers but from within the religious world and the Church! God tells His people in Judges 3 to watch out because He's deliberately allowed these opponents to be right in our face to teach us how to fight spiritually. Remember: we never fight people – people are never our enemy! We do however have to learn from Ephesians 6 how to fight spiritually and win; then we need to settle in our souls that, as Churchill said, "we will never give in, never give in, never, never, never, never; we will never yield to the apparently overwhelming might of the enemy!"

If those first two don't rock your confidence, then beware of the third whammy! God's *"delays"* really deeply test our "ways". It's as if He's turned out the lights and gone on holiday, as He is just not responding to our calls! Now before we feel picked on, remember that Moses had this treatment, so did Abraham, and so did our young shepherd/soldier David – even Jesus had to endure through these times of silence, delay, and zero response.

Jesus expected to take off into ministry when he reached the age of thirteen after his Bar Mitzvah. Remarkably his Father

God was silent when his earthly parents failed to understand His mission, and Jesus just embraced the 17-year delay and submitted obediently to them until he was 30 and reached the age of inheritance. Wow! That is some delay! It was however identical to the wait that Joseph endured, as he waited for the fulfillment of his dream for 17 years, enduring betrayal, seduction, false charges, prison, and silence!

What we need to capture from this story in Luke 2:52, is that Jesus "grew in wisdom, stature and favour with both God and men" throughout this time of submitting to his parents and waiting for God's timing - and He didn't even have the power of the Holy Spirit resting on Him and flowing through Him as we do today. The truth is that, through these times of delay, something deeply surrenders on the inside and we come to such a place of "brokenness" before God that truly we are now "safe to be used." It costs God dearly as a Father to painfully watch us navigate these times of inner fight and frustration in the times of delay. What is at stake however is that viral Kingdom: by any means, He will ensure that you and I are fashioned and shaped through these times to become those contagious carriers of His viral Kingdom.

I mentioned earlier in the transformation process, that "desperation leads us to revelation": this time of delay has the potential to become the seedbed of so much divine revelation so that we can come through it with totally different spiritual eyesight. Throughout the Bible, God keeps asking the same question: "What are you seeing with your spiritual eyes?". He keeps asking the prophets, because once they "see" it, He's able to carry out whatever He's promised. These times open up our inner spiritual eyes of faith so that we can see in the invisible realm. This in turn enables us to attempt the impossible – because we've seen it! Paul tells the Ephesians that he's constantly praying for them during this time of spiritual warfare, so that the inner "eyes of their hearts might be opened".

We started by comparing the ways in which both David and Jesus were trained into Kingdom thinking. Both, like Joseph, struggled through those silent years, knowing they were "God's chosen" as well as "God's anointed and appointed." There is such a remarkable flow of Grace shown in all three, together with such a tenderness and brokenness; we can only respond in humility and ask God to work this Grace in each one of us for the sake of His Kingdom, "Lord! Let you Kingdom come!"

CHAPTER 5

SO HOW DOES THIS KINGDOM OPERATE?

The tax collector Matthew has his life totally turned around by Jesus and the new dimension of the Kingdom of God. He is now part of this beachhead group of apostles and disciples which has established itself, following the atomic impact of Jesus giving his life as a sacrifice on the Cross: this decimated the demonic powers and principalities which had ruled unchallenged since time began. So now this tax collector becomes the collector of any story that he can lay his hands on, so that he can tell the world about this invasion of the Kingdom of God into our world.

This is the main passion of Matthew's book, the first book of the New Testament. He mentions the Kingdom far more than any of the other apostles, because he can see that his normal business thinking is diametrically opposed to Kingdom thinking, in fact almost the opposite. He can see that there are so many human solutions and projects which are opposite to a Kingdom mindset. So, he sets himself to analyze the attitudes and principles of the Kingdom and recognizes that the only way to see the Kingdom is through the total surrender of his life to Jesus. He knows that he must lay aside his business thinking, even his religious training, and become like a little child in terms of child-like simplicity and faith, before he can enter this realm of the Kingdom.

He records story after story of how Jesus demonstrates the Kingdom, and how the devil hates it. We see him recording how Jesus makes a declaration of war against the dominion of demonic darkness as he proclaims the Kingdom, noting down some of the salutary lessons from the life of John the Baptist: anything representing the Kingdom will be attacked, and sadly we see John losing his life in his confusion and inability to recognize who Jesus really is. Matthew then records how Jesus stops to honour John - "throughout history there has never been anyone who surpassed John"- but then he shocks everyone with this statement: "but I tell you that the least of those who now experience this new Kingdom realm will be greater than my friend John! *Something greater has now arrived!*" (Matt 11)

What a remarkable statement! Jesus doesn't put *himself* forward and say that *"someone* greater has arrived"; he is heralding the dawn of *"something* totally new" - a new era – the D-Day (to use the war analogy) of the spiritual forces representing the invasion of the Kingdom of God. On those spiritual Omaha beaches of this Kingdom invasion against the forces of darkness, John sacrificed his life along with many others since that time, who proclaimed it but never saw it. We owe an eternal debt of gratitude to those early pioneers of the faith who laid their lives down to make way for the inbreaking waves of the Kingdom of God.

Matthew continues to unpack the mysteries of this new realm, announcing it as a totally new culture which is not going to mesh with the old. This "new wine" needs a brand new "wineskin". The catch is this: if you can "see" it, you will get it, if you don't, you won't. It's that simple and revolutionary. Matthew shows Peter shouting out "I can see it now! You're the Christ! You're what this whole Kingdom is about!" That one flash of revelation is the key which enabled him, and now enables us, to see the Kingdom realm.

For those from the generation of the Matrix film, you'll understand the cry, "just take the red pill!" Taking that red pill – in Kingdom terms, allowing the blood of Jesus to wash and cleanse our hearts, minds and perception – only this will allow us to perceive the realm of the Kingdom, because it is invisible to the human eye.

So Matthew records the catalogue of stories that Jesus uses to try to explain these spiritual truths to those with an open hungry teachable heart. He makes it very clear however that there are two completely different realms here, and the dividing line is determined by one thing only – the state of people's hearts. People are either "in or out"; they are either "wheat or weeds", either "open and receptive to the Word" or "closed, confused or cluttered". There is no middle ground. History and destiny are decided for each individual by the response of their heart to the Kingdom.

One of the things which shocks us, is the way two different kingdoms are set against each other - the Kingdom of God and the kingdom of the spirit behind money (Mammon). We must choose who will govern our lives, and the reality is that this wicked spirit of Mammon controls the lives and thinking of vast portions of the world, and even sometimes of the church. Jesus even calls his Kingdom message a "Gospel for the poor" because it is so hard for the rich to break away from that controlling spirit. Three times in my life God has told me to give away everything and just trust Him, because I was becoming more and more dependent on what I had in the bank account, rather than depending on Him. The power of that spirit is evident in retrospect in that having obeyed God each of those times, it wasn't long before I found myself controlled again by fear and anxiety in the financial realm. It is a wicked spirit that confronts the Lordship of Christ in our lives.

Matthew uses so much of his book to unpack the secrets of the Kingdom through more stories so that we can begin to recognize the Kingdom. If it's "Kingdom" it will grow, even if it seems so small; it will attract, influence, gather, and protect. This unseen spiritual force will spread virally, and it will permeate everything. Since it is so valuable it will be hidden, and we will have to search for it with all of our heart (Jer 29:13) God's mercy and salvation can simply be *received*, but we have to make every effort to *find* Grace and the Kingdom (Heb 4:16)

The key however which unlocks this Kingdom is "faith", which we will deal with in a later chapter. This is the only ingredient which activates the seed: faith is the germination of that seed of God's Word in the womb of our spirit. It is our total commitment to what God has said: it's all or nothing. Faith is our willingness to give up everything we have, to have Him and trust Him, and it is "gambling our all on the faithfulness of God."

Sacrifice however is the trigger at every level: God the Father sacrificed his Son and was willing to give us everything; Jesus sacrificed His life and poured out everything for us; the Holy Spirit then sacrifices and sets himself apart exclusively for us. Romans 12 says: "In view of all God's sacrificial mercy" let us then offer our bodies up to him as a living sacrifice to activate the work of the Spirit and the Kingdom through our lives. There could be no higher calling!

At the heart of this intimate Kingdom relationship is the "Sower and the Seed" (the Father sowing His Son, the Word of God). Our part in all of this is the state of the "soil" of our hearts, and our willingness to "sacrifice". Our reaction to the Word - both decision and action - will determine whether that "Seed" can penetrate our hearts. When it does, God sends His "Sanctifier" - the Holy Spirit - to seal it in our hearts, germinate, grow and complete what He's promised. This is why the most important parable of Jesus is the parable of the Sower: every other parable hangs on this, because it shows the state of the soil of our heart, which will either be:

- » closed and hardened - wounded, calloused and impenetrable
- » open but wounded - so shallow that trouble and persecution will rob this seed
- » open but cluttered - overwhelmed by worries, anxieties, leisure, pleasure, or wealth

» open and prepared - receiving, understanding, and planting that word, then holding on to it, persevering until it finally gives birth and the Word becomes "flesh".

Whether we like it or not, both God and Satan will be able to sow into our hearts. Our hearts are like an open field and so we are told, above every other priority, to make sure that we guard our heart otherwise the "wellspring of life" will get blocked up. (Prov 4:23). This is the most important thing in our life – as I said, the priority God gives it is "above everything else!" God is warning us that moments of trauma and pain will come to us personally when cracks may appear in the wounded soil of our heart. It is at those times that we need to guard the field of our hearts.

If we are rejected, beware of those seeds of anger and insecurity which may be sown into our heart, leaving an abandoned and orphan spirit; if we are abused, beware of those seeds of fear and anxiety and even self-hatred; if we are criticized and judged harshly, we need to be careful that we don't internalize it into a self-rejection, unable to receive love, or accept our self and our gifting. If we are controlled, the enemy may so easily sow into that wound his seeds of rebellion, lying, cheating and deception. This is no game – it is a fight to the death, as the enemy seeks to drive you back off the beachhead of inner Kingdom peace, hope and joy.

The most wicked, deceptive and mean thing of all is that the devil then accuses you of the very seeds he's sown! You start believing the lie that this is what you are like. No! Rom 7:20 says so clearly that it's not you! It is those demonic seeds of sin which the devil has sown inside you during those painful times of wounding. Don't let the devil get a foothold, otherwise he will slowly develop a stronghold on the inside of you which will begin to rob you of any Kingdom faith. Many of the Kingdom warriors pushing forward into the enemy's territory may be "saved" but they may well not be free inside: they may have allowed themselves to become wounded leaders who nurse insecurities and these wicked seeds of the enemy, and they may end up in turn wounding and hurting others. "Friendly fire" has taken out countless numbers of God's Kingdom forces. We will deal with this in detail in the coming chapters.

CHAPTER 6

THE HEART OF THE MATTER

As soon as he can, our tax-collector Matthew goes for the jugular: "You want to know the truth about the Kingdom? Well let me tell you then about the Kingdom Manifesto! The whole heart of the matter is the matter of the heart – you need to know the type of heart which will be ready to embrace and grow those divine Kingdom seeds". He captures a glimpse of Jesus on a hillside, deeply involved in communicating to his team about the core cultural values of this new Kingdom, which they are seeking to release virally wherever they go. He starts with core values that are completely opposite to what they are thinking:

"These are the types of attitudes which you need to look for if we are going to multiply and spread this Kingdom. We need people who are willing to admit that they are spiritually bankrupt – even barren and powerless – who are not spiritually blind and deceived people who think that they they've got it all together. We need those who are not afraid to display a bit of inner turmoil and desperation, like Hannah - Samuel's mother - when she was groaning in prayer clinging on to God's promise of a child. These people are so desperate that they will not be silenced, and they carry their heart cry openly.

Then we need those with a "tender strength"- soft in God's hands – who carry a gentleness and humility; those too who are yearning and craving, with a deep spiritual hunger for a restored relationship with God. Above all, we need those whose hearts are prepared to be open conduits of all the love and grace they receive from God, who will not only draw on the mercy of God but will pass it on to all they meet. They will be people who are not complex but show a simplicity and purity of heart which will motivate them to radiate love with a good conscience and sincere faith, with no traces of bitterness and unforgiveness.

We need peacemakers too - they are a unique breed - who are like the oil in a creaking door, always dedicated to pouring balm on wounded relationships, and reconnecting the disconnected, and who will never rest in prayer until they have brought broken people back to peace and reconciliation. Finally, we need some Kingdom-minded people who just say, "bring it on!" when the going gets tough and all kinds of slurs and accusations are flying around, because they know that people are never their enemy, and they know full well that they are rattling the devils cage!"

What an extraordinary Kingdom manifesto! Mathew then tries to boil the Kingdom down into four characteristic ways in which it is manifested. He tells us that it's going to be "like salt, but also like light - like leaven but also like a city". Like the tiny grains of salt, this Kingdom culture is going to bring out the different flavours in society, as well as acting as a brake to stop the rot and preserve our core values. It will permeate society with love, joy, and peace, infiltrating every sphere and strata of society. It will allow righteousness to filter through to all levels of local and national government, because it is only righteousness which will exalt a Nation. However, if we lose this salty culture we cannot expect the church to be immune to a backlash, when society kicks back at the Church and tramples it under foot.

This Kingdom culture will also manifest with a characteristic of light which will contrast with and confront systems of darkness, injustice and oppression. It will create radiant examples and models of Kingdom schools, companies, businesses, hospitals, medical practices, and families – all carrying, and unapologetically displaying, Kingdom values at every level.

We should then anticipate the steady growth and viral permeation of this Kingdom culture to be like leaven which almost imperceptibly spreads virally through the dough until every part is affected, and its level is raised. In contrast to this viral spread, the Kingdom will also manifest in a way similar to the characteristics of a city set on a hill which cannot be hidden. It will develop power centres of prayer and worship hubs, which will demonstrate the unbridled power and authority of the Kingdom, where declarations will be made which will change whole districts, communities, and Nations. The Kingdom in all its Glory has yet to be manifested like this, to the extent that the Church is no longer robbed, silenced or neutralized.

I think of the moment in San Antonio when a Kingdom group of pastors and intercessors gathered with my father-in law as a modern-day "tabernacle of David", specifically to confront Hurricane Lili as it sought to devastate the southern seaboard of Texas. They were all under His command as they worshipped all night until God released a powerful authority on the meeting at 9.15pm. At that point the Holy Spirit directed them to face Hurricane Lili and command it to stop! The meteorological website the next day spoke of the mystery of why, at 9.15pm the night before, Hurricane Lili just died and dropped to a whimper of wind. Now that's our God!

That is the unbridled manifestation of the Kingdom power which we need to grow in! We are called to be "Royal Intercessors" who make decrees in the spirit world which will dramatically change situations: sadly, the church in the West has largely lost this art, and often prays weak and ineffective pleading prayers. Matthew shouts out from his book that with even a mustard seed of Kingdom faith we can move mountains! "Nothing will be impossible for you!"

If you and I seriously want to manifest this level of power and authority, then something radical needs to take place. For a start we need to get rid of all triumphalism and recognize that these things are humanly impossible: we cannot do this! None of our external activity or structures will come anywhere near this level of Kingdom manifestation. However, as we surrender to his mercy and grace and give ourselves unceasingly to Him from a base of heart unity, humility, and prayer – then anything is possible!

Very briefly, scouring through the Bible, we can catch a few flickers of this Kingdom power breaking forth. Right from the original model of the Kingdom in the garden of Eden, we become aware of what God has in mind for the Kingdom. There are four rivers which flow out of Eden which symbolize the life flow which God envisages from His Kingdom - Pishon, Gihon, Tigris, and Euphrates. The four names of these rivers mean "increase", "bursting forth", "rapid", and "fruitfulness". What a different picture that conjures up about what God had in mind for His Kingdom. Then in Daniel 2 we see that God intends His Kingdom to "fill, subdue and crush" every other kingdom that comes in its way.

In the New Testament we are then gripped with different illustrations, showing that the Kingdom will be like leaven which will permeate everything. It may look as insignificant as a mustard seed, but it will spread and grow rapidly until it fills the whole earth. Finally, God shows the Kingdom in its true, uncontained and unlimited character of wild fire which sweeps through the Nations.

The Kingdom is not a place or even a sphere, but it is a contagious relational network. Jesus says that it is "something" – a heavenly virus - which gets into us, and this Kingdom takes us over. God rules and God directs - no questions and qualifications, and only *total obedience* will lead us into the perfect will of God. So much of our western religious Christianity is "knowledge based", with constant pressure to "know more", do another course, or obtain another degree. This is utterly alien to those simple early "ignorant and unlearned" disciples, for whom the Kingdom was totally "faith and obedience based".

We make a life decision to allow Jesus' unconditional love to rule our lives, so that we can dedicate ourselves to a lifestyle of forgiveness in which we are empowered to rescue people throughout our lives, because it's His Word which is inside us. It is His passion and zeal which consumes us. Truly, as Jeremiah said, "we have fire in our bones!" This is the "heavenly virus" which I have dedicated my life to pursue, compelled by God's Spirit – a force so infectious and contagious that it can only be carried by those who have clung to the Cross long enough for their inner ego and "little me" to be truly crucified so that they no longer live but the Christ-Kingdom anointing lives in them in power!

So where is this Kingdom thinking today? I have been privileged to witness its revival fire sweeping through parts of Africa and Asia, and especially China, as I have worked alongside men like Brother Yun, the Heavenly Man, and Reinhard Bonnke; but God is no respecter of places and has no favorites. In my spirit I have wrestled with God, with His fire burning through me as He persistently asked me "Why won't you believe me for 30 million Muslims?" It took me almost an hour to surrender, and scream "OK! 30 million Muslims!" I stood up with a seed of living faith within me that we will see this in our day. This is just for starters! The Muslim world will come to know the "man in white" of their dreams and come to know "Isa Al-Masih (Jesus the Messiah) as their Lord and their Saviour!

God cannot be limited, and I believe "Fortress Europe" is also about to be shaken with the fire of God! The Ice Age of secularism, materialism, religion, and the globalist agendas have prepared the ground to such an extent that a cry is now rising from these Nations: "Show us your God! Show us the Kingdom in all its Power and Glory!" There is a wild radical generation who are yet to be ignited with the fire of God, and they will sweep through these Nations demonstrating the Kingdom of God. We've lingered too long in passive self-indulgence, focusing on the face of the Father and the Bridegroom; it's time to lay down our rights, get into rank, and report for duty and be gripped by the face of our Lord and our King! God, let your Kingdom come in power! Send your Holy Spirit for the sake of your Kingdom!

CHAPTER 7

IT'S FIRE WE PRAY, IT'S FIRE WE NEED!

"It's fire we pray, it's fire we need: send your fire!" These were the words that the early Salvation Army sang, day after day, as they pioneered one of the greatest moves of God in the UK to reach the broken and the marginalized. William Booth, totally in the face of the culture of his day, refused to recognize gender differences, and some of his most outstanding leaders and evangelists were young women. Somehow, over the generations, many of their churches and leaders lost that fire, but there is a fresh wind of the Spirit blowing through the Salvation Army today, as they cry out to God again for His fire.

The bottom line is this: "No sacrifice – no fire!" You will see throughout this book that this is an underlying theme. In view of all God's mercy, what else can we do in response, but put our lives on that altar as living sacrifices, holy and pleasing to Him. We see Jesus in Luke 12 telling them: "Come on! I have come to bring fire on the earth and oh how I wish it was already on fire and viral; but there's something I have to do before it goes viral, and my soul is in absolute turmoil until that happens - I have to embrace the ultimate personal sacrifice on the Cross. So, don't think I've just come to give you a peaceful ride! This requires personal sacrifice, carrying your own cross, and this will be the dividing line for so many of you".

Jesus knows the principle that the fire will only fall on sacrifice – both His and ours. In the upper room as He comes to that moment of sacrificing His life, He knows that He needs to infect His disciples with the same fire and glory that He carries. He breaks bread and covenantally imparts His life and infects them with this "heavenly virus" of the Kingdom. He then shouts out in prayer, "I've done it! I have given them the Kingdom!"- but how?

One thing that we need to see here is the reason why Jesus can operate with such authority and power and transfer it to us - even before He has been to the Cross and destroyed the devil's kingdom. The reason is that Jesus operates as a man within the constraints of "human chronos time"; however, in his spirit He knows that God exists outside of "chronos time" and He knows that "the Lamb has already been slain before the foundation of the world". He operates on earth with something my father in law called a "Kingdom credit card" knowing that the bill is already paid in eternity before the foundation of the world. The blood of the Lamb has already been shed and He is trustfully handing over His Kingdom "credit card" to all his disciples. Obviously, after the Crucifixion and Pentecost, they no longer need this Kingdom "credit card" as it is then an established fact in "chronos time": this explains why they can legally do all that they have done in signs and wonders - even before the battle is over.

There is an unshakable Jesus culture that we can release by laying our lives down: this is the "Jesus culture" which spreads contagiously like a virus. Even though the vast proportion of Muslims are just nominal and peace loving, real Islam uses the principle and medium of "sacrifice", but with a totally different spirit. Within every Christian there is this latent seed of "sacrifice", which is often never germinated due to our leisure/pleasure/comfort Christian world. However, if you throw these same people into the furnace of intense persecution and opposition, that latent seed is often germinated, and a revival fire of life and hope is ignited.

Just read of the China revival, as well as many other like the Naga revival in Nagaland. This is the story in countless nations where the church has been persecuted. Sadly, within every Muslim there is also a counterfeit seed of "sacrifice" or "jihad". We need to beware: if you throw these precious people into the intense fire of persecution and opposition, that seed of "jihad" is often germinated, resulting in a wave of death and despair, with senseless self-sacrifice and human carnage.

Young people today are looking for something radical. They are looking for something that is worthy of laying their lives down. Religion will crush and control them, but this radical sacrificial Kingdom life is uncontrollable, and viral! The trouble is, that in western Christianity we have often been guilty of concealing this dimension of "sacrifice" because we don't want people to be weird and over the top. This has locked millions on the first side of the Cross, where Jesus is rightly portrayed as the one on the Cross who died in our place: it's all about us - we've been forgiven, freed from slavery to sin, healed and delivered, and reconciled to the Father! On this side of the Cross, we see the face of the Father, and fall in love with Jesus as our Bridegroom. Peter even says that we have the right of access to everything that we need through the incredible promises God has made to us. It is fantastic, it is mind-blowing, but *this is for us*, and it's not enough to change the world if we keep it to ourselves. The later chapters are dedicated to unpack and explain all of these aspects of the Cross.

Many Christians never cross over to the other side of the Cross because they have never been told about it! I certainly wasn't and had to find it years later. You see, the other side of the Cross *is no longer about me*, it's about Christ and His Kingdom. On this other side of the Cross, it's "little me" on the Cross with Jesus: "Little me" has to be crucified with Christ and "little me" can no longer live thinking it's all about me. Like Jesus in Phil 2, I have to surrender all my rights even though I have the right of access to everything! I have to be willing to become a servant and humble myself even to the point of personal sacrifice. God is no longer just my Father and certainly Jesus is not just my Bridegroom: now He's my Lord and my King!

This is where I get clothed with the uniform of Christ. I become a soldier under command, falling in rank with thousands of others waiting to obey the Lord's command. This is where we become channels of the Kingdom power, glory and love, compelled by an explosion of His love within us through the power and authority of the Holy Spirit. We are now carrying the "heavenly virus"- His fire - because this virus is activated the moment we put "little me" on the Cross and surrender our lives into the Kingdom. This is what I mean by the "Jesus culture". It is unstoppable, and it is also our weapon of warfare.

Peter says in his first letter (chapter 4): "Look, remember the weapon Jesus used as He suffered in His body and embraced the Cross: that attitude of willingness to suffer and sacrifice is a weapon. It will seriously mess with all your own selfish desires and cause you to become almost obsessed with one thing - to be right at the centre of God's plan and will. So, pick up this weapon and use it: get ready, be prepared, be alert, be self-controlled and be totally separated from all the other distractions in your life. Be a radical, and don't let the enemy intimidate you!" Let me tell you, the moment you sign up for the Kingdom like this, all hell will come against you. However, just learn to surf the waves of opposition rolling in on you and refuse to be submerged by it into Christian mediocrity and ineffectiveness.

God says to you: "I know the devil is raging against me and against you my anointed ones, but listen: "you are my legal sons and heirs. Think big or you will limit me: ask me for Nations!" - this is the size and scope of the inheritance Jesus has won on that Cross and has given to you. As I said in an earlier chapter, each of us has to fight our own battle in the wilderness - just as Jesus did - to establish our own personal right to be clothed with the uniform of His power and authority so that we can advance God's invisible Kingdom on earth, carrying His unstoppable "heavenly virus". So, the global battle is on, and this could be our finest hour!

As we forget past defeats and failures, let's fix our eyes on Jesus, the triumphant King of Kings and Lord of Lords, but also the one who not only infects us with His faith but enables us to complete the impossible tasks He gives us. Let's also learn from Peter and those first Kingdom warriors and learn from all that they faced. As the Bible says, all these stories are written down as examples and warnings for us in this generation.

From that first flush of Kingdom explosion at Pentecost, there was an immediate breakthrough. Suddenly, they not only had the power but they also had the authority over demonic principalities and powers. What followed was a time of fearless proclamation of the name of Jesus with signs and wonders being demonstrated, and many demonic powers were broken and cast out. The whole of the Roman Empire was impacted over the next 30 years! But wait - then the intense persecution began under Emperor Nero: all the apostles were killed, Peter was just about to be martyred, and it really looked on the surface that the devil was winning. The kingdom of darkness seemed to have triumphed in its backlash, because only a few weak remnants of Kingdom warriors were struggling to survive.

This was the background when Peter sat down and wrote his two letters to the Churches. In his first letter he majors on the external persecution which will always strengthen and purify the church, and it will somehow create in us a holiness, purity, faith and hope to endure through all the suffering. China is a prime example of this. However, his second letter is very sobering. It is this letter which applies to us today in the western nations: he focusses on the internal infiltration of worldliness, deception, and compromise which can lead to the destruction of the church. It is this internal infiltration that brings weakness and defeats us!

Peter writes his letters to the church in a time just like today, and what is remarkable is that these letters release an unshakeable faith into the church. It is a faith that causes believers to see in the invisible realm that "we are condemned to victory in Christ!" Those who come to see in the invisible realm have the faith and courage to attempt the impossible. Peter was utterly convinced that God was going to do what He had promised, and that the Kingdom of God would break through. He knew that Jesus would come again one day in mighty power and that His reign would be established on earth.

Three years later, the apostle John comes to Ephesus during Nero's persecution. He stays for 12 years, but then John is exiled to Patmos for 15 years, where he finally receives his revelations. John is unshakable but says to the church in Ephesus: "I know how hard you are working in the Kingdom, and I also know how much you've had to push through and persevere, but there's one thing which you've got wrong - you have forgotten your first love and intimacy with the Lord." This was John's solid rock and this needs to be the anchor for our souls too. Even today, most mornings I will drop to my knees in gratitude and thank the Lord for his incredible covenant with me and my family - I will break bread (not religiously) and begin to make declarations over different situations: this is an anchor for my soul.

During these next 30 years the church went through almost a literal "hell on earth", and this prepared the church for the explosive radical fire of the "Jesus culture". What the devil doesn't understand is this: when he tries to kill Jesus, incredible power is released on that Cross which totally disarms him. Then when the devil tries to kill the church, a "heavenly virus" is released of radical sacrificial "life laid down" faith that is unstoppable! Peter's message is so relevant to this generation because dark clouds of secularism, atheism, and religion are threatening the church globally. In some nations it seems that the devil wants to stamp out real Kingdom faith, and it looks as if we are losing the battle. This is where we need to stand up, and "face the facts, but not fuel the fear." Often these places of the fiercest battle are the next landing ground for a supernatural revival of the Holy Spirit.

Just to give you the good news: there is a final showdown in Ephesus, when John aged 90 is released from Patmos. He comes to Ephesus with the fire of God burning in him: he marches into the temple of Artemis/Diana and confronts the principality and powers which ruled that area of Asia. History records that the altar splits in two and half the temple falls down! With immediate effect the power of that demonic spirit is broken and within 50 years, Diana worship is extinct. Wow! That is some authority! Ephesus then becomes the centre for advancing the Kingdom for 200 years! We will come back to all this history in the last chapter, so that we can learn vital lessons.

If you compare this with modern-day China, it is so similar: they experienced 30 years of crucifixion from 1950 to 1980 after Mao closed down all the churches. Then in the next 30 years from 1980 to 2010, the church experienced unprecedented and explosive growth as the fire of revival spread like wildfire across China through the Holy Spirit which the authorities couldn't stop! The cycle is beginning again right now and the church in China is experiencing intense and sustained persecution and harassment. They need our prayer! This demonic persecution from certain sectors of the current Chinese government is destined to release one of the greatest missionary movements in history!

PART TWO

②

UNDERSTANDING CHRIST'S CROSS

CHAPTER 8

THE FOOLISHNESS OF THE CROSS

So, with all these thoughts in our minds and before you begin reading this next section about the Cross, please do take some time to ask God to make this a direct revelation to your spirit. To be honest, if this is just an academic study for you, then this could be just information and not revelation. Revelation will go straight to your spirit and change you, way beyond the natural power of my written words. "So Father, we want to thank you for the power of the Cross, and we pray that the Spirit of God would just impact each one of us individually where we're at, and that revelation would come to our spirits. We pray that it wouldn't just be a mental exercise, but that revelation would come to each one of us."

Listen to the heart of Paul's message in Corinth: "For Christ didn't send me to baptize, but to preach the Gospel - not with words of human wisdom *lest the Cross of Christ be emptied of its power. For the message of the Cross is foolishness to those who are perishing but to us who are being saved, it is the power of God.*" (1 Cor 1:17-18) He goes on to say: "For I resolved to know nothing while I was with you, except Jesus Christ and Him crucified. I came to you in weakness and fear and with much trembling. My message and my preaching were not with wise and persuasive words but *with a demonstration of the Spirit's power, so that your faith may not rest on men's wisdom but on God's power.*" (1 Cor 2: 2-5)

Let me give you some background as to why Paul wrote this letter to the Corinthians. Paul is passionate: he is so zealous that he just wants to sweep right through the whole of Asia minor with the Gospel. Paul wants to travel all the way up to Ephesus and neutralize that demonic stronghold which rules Asia Minor through the spirit of Artemis/Diana. Strangely however we read in Acts 16 that when he tries to get into Asia, "the spirit of Christ stopped him"- Jesus just stops him in his tracks! Instead, Paul receives a call from God to go to Europe - over to Macedonia. So, this effectively takes Paul on a "walkabout", travelling through five different cities, not understanding what this was all about. All that time, God is wrestling with Paul's intellect because he hasn't yet come to understand the full realm of the Spirit and he needs to understand spiritual warfare.

Paul must come to understand the power of the Cross: he has to understand the full victory of that Cross and see that it wasn't just "Jesus on the Cross" taking the penalty of all our sin. The reach and impact of the Cross would send shock waves through the whole spirit world, signalling an end to the devil's control and domination of the whole of mankind. On this journey, Paul comes to understand the journey through the stages of the Cross and realises that the Cross is now transformed into Christs "sword of victory".

He needs to see the practical application of the power of the Cross in these different cities. In each of these cities he experiences first-hand how the demonic and religious worlds operate and how to respond without being intimidated or neutralized. In Philippi he casts out a demon and ends up in prison: but he responds with faith and praises God at midnight- an earthquake breaks open the prison, Paul and his friends are free, and the jailor and his family get saved – not bad for his first lesson of faith on this "walkabout"! Then he goes on to Thessalonica and preaches on the Cross and has an amazing revival in just three weeks. It causes such a demonic reaction that he is arrested. Somehow he escapes and ends up in Berea where his preaching has the same impact; however, he soon realizes that religious territorial spirits work together to close down the Gospel: they come to take him out, but Paul gives them the slip and moves to his next lesson.

Paul arrives in a very intellectual city called Athens. He is in Athens as an intellectual: he thinks he can play their game and so he plays their intellectual game. He begins to start debating with them and ends the debate by talking about Jesus in intellectual terms. Absolutely nothing happens! There is no riot, and there is no revival, as there had been in the first two cities. Normally that's what happens when the power of Cross is proclaimed in all its majesty: there's often a riot but there's also a revival.

Paul feels really puzzled, as his preaching does not have any impact at all in Athens. So, he assesses "what is going on here": it was fruitless, and it was powerless. Sadly, what they were gripped by in Athens is exactly what we're gripped by in Oxford and in our society: it's humanism, and all the other "isms" that just grip our minds. Paul realizes: "I've got to change, I can't preach this message intellectually". He then has to walk all the way from Athens to Corinth and you can imagine that on this journey he is wrestling with God. "God why did nothing happen? What happened Father? Father, please tell me." And so, God begins to show him the foolishness of his ways and begins to show him that he can no longer preach as an intellectual - he has to change his whole life message.

Praise God, because from that moment onwards, Paul resolves to know nothing but "Jesus Christ and Him crucified", which is what he preached in the first two cities. By the time he arrives in Corinth, he's thinking "I'm going to go for it. I've got the message now! This message is not going to be effective just because I'm an intellectual. *This message itself is the power of God!* I simply need to preach the message of the Cross and not rationalize with people and wrestle with their intellectual thoughts. I must simply preach the message of Jesus Christ and Him crucified." So that is exactly what he did: Paul simply comes in weakness and he preaches the power of God.

Paul declares to them, "Listen with your spirits, don't just listen to my words. The power of God is moving here!" People are being healed and there is tremendous power being released in Corinth. The Spirit of God is at last free to move. You see, if we are gripped by humanism or rationalism, what happens in the Church is that it slowly begins to take on "a form of religion which denies the power of God" (2 Tim 3-5). We come to a place where people refuse absolutes, and they begin to make everything very relative. Everything becomes "synthetic thinking". The Bible is never synthetic - it's never relative - it is black and white! We have to change our thinking and think biblically.

I've realized this truth over the years: that if we preach "the old Cross", we will get "the old power". If we preach a watered-down Cross, we get little power. That is what we hear in so many places - a watered-down cross. The Cross has become so sanitized, so sentimental, and so plastic. I think we all know deep down, that it was a gruesome act - it was awful! We cannot sentimentalize the Cross, so we must recognize the awfulness of what really happened on that Cross. It truly cost God everything! I mean this - God lost everything. "God who did not even withhold his son, will he not freely with him give us all things" (Rom 8) He knows that it is going to cost Him everything, and yet even then He also wants to give us everything else in addition!

God wants so much to give us the Kingdom, which is why we must beware of the deceptive message of the "new cross": it is very subtle. We must beware of creating a culture of "constant counselling", as if this is the key to freedom. Yes, I do a lot of counselling, and as a Pastor it is only right to spend a lot of time helping people through their problems. However, we must be very careful of some kinds of counselling which minimize the impact of the Cross, because "flesh is flesh". Much humanistic-inspired "Christian" counselling just tends to rearrange the flesh, without getting to the root of the problem.

Listen - "counselling that does not lead people to the Cross is not effective Christian counselling!" People need to come to the Cross, because that is the only place where they will be set free. As a counsellor, you will soon see that flesh can very easily clothe itself in religion: it can look pretty - it can look religious - it can even look holy. Sadly, it is still the flesh. Jesus did not come to "improve" our lives. He came to "remove" the domination of the "little old me" from our lives. So, the Cross is about God removing that dominant "little me" out of the scene. So often when we are in counselling, we're trying to improve people's lives rather than bringing them to the Cross. We need to say, "listen, this area of your self-life has to die." We know about the Cross, but few are willing to die to themselves. If we can bring people to this moment of surrender, suddenly they will be free, and they will be able to walk free: they can be "new creations"!

Too many people rearrange the flesh and end up with the same old problems. We must allow the Cross to do its work. I remember in Northern Ireland when I was wrestling with all this as a soldier, struggling with PTSD after 4 of my soldiers were killed. I was wrestling with so many things in my own personal life, but I just kept on pulling out the "weak and pathetic" card. I had been to counselling, but I just came out feeling exactly the same: "I'm just weak and pathetic, I've got this problem and I've got all these other problems." I remember somebody looking at me straight in the face and speaking very slowly to me - it was like a slap in the face to wake me up! He said: "listen, the Cross cannot and will not work for you if you're just seeing yourself as "weak and pathetic".

Until you can say "I'm guilty!", the Cross will not be able to help you. You have to confess by facing the facts and then take responsibility for the guilt of what you've allowed to be sown into your life. Stop this self-pity and just admit to God: "God I am so sorry! I know that I'm guilty of allowing this fear into my life." Instantly the blood will touch you, and you will be free!" Now that talk was a turning point in my life.

I have found this again and again in counselling, even with people who have been brutally wounded or who've been badly abused: as long as they remain "victims" in their mentality, they find it so difficult to get free. However, the moment they put their hands up and say, "Father, I am so sorry for what I allowed to be sown into my life during that traumatic time," God begins to set them free and heal them. It's important to remember that we're not saying sorry for what has happened to us - of course, all these things are unbelievably painful!

However, we are saying sorry to God for what we have allowed to come into our hearts, because our heart is the wellspring of life. We personally have to guard our heart: that is absolutely clear from Proverbs - we have to guard our heart. I have found again and again that as soon as people say "Father, I'm so sorry that I've harboured this resentment, and I've had this anger" - instantly they're free of feelings that have gripped them for years. However, if they walk around the wilderness keeping a "victim mentality", they seldom get free. So, we must recognise the Cross: it is gruesome, but it is effective. Once you see it in your spirit, you will never want to mess around again with sin. You've finally seen what it cost Jesus!

We cannot save people through a liberal compromising message. Truth that sets people free is black or white - it's right or wrong. Paul remembers his failure in Athens and as he begins walking from Athens to Corinth, God begins to speak to him about the power of the Cross and the potential for breakthrough if people will just apply it. Suddenly Paul gets this revelation, and he finally "sees" the power of the Cross. "That's it! This is what is going to set people free!" And that is why by the time he arrives in Corinth, he changes his whole message. It is only a revelation of the Cross that will set us free. I knew about the Cross for years, but I never had the revelation which would enable me to personally apply the Cross to my life. Truth is spiritually discerned, and it is not intellectually worked out.

It is spiritually discerned: so, as we begin this whole process of unlocking the Cross, may I just plead with each of us not to try to work it out intellectually. Pray with me: "Father, show me something today. Give me a revelation of this in my spirit. I want to see this!" We need to put our minds on the altar, and put our whole being on the altar. God says in Romans 12: 2, "Come on! Don't be conformed any longer to the pattern of this world's thinking, but be transformed by the renewing of your mind." We must have our minds renewed, which means that we start thinking "God thoughts". I know it is so easy to think the way of the world, but "God's thoughts are not our thoughts". Allow the Spirit of God to unlock this for you.

We must also beware of trusting our human words of wisdom, or even our human theology. The Cross will be at the very centre of this book, so I'm believing that this may enable each one of us to "take up our cross daily and follow Him". It is through our daily walk with Jesus that He will lead us into fully understanding the Cross. I have been in "evangelical circles" for many years and have watched so many people come to the Cross as a theology, without actually experiencing its freedom. No! We must take up our cross, understanding that it's a daily reality. We must understand that the key is in the fact that the Cross is working in us and through us daily. It is the key to knowing we are truly "saved", but it is also the key to keep on "being saved" in the future.

May I gently confront one myth before we continue: it is the myth about "signs and wonders". I have witnessed so many great healing miracles, but in themselves they do not transform people's lives spiritually. They are wonderful, wonderful gifts from God, but "transformation happens at the Cross." We see signs, wonders, miracles and healings all the time, but it is the personal application of the work of the Cross which actively does something deep inside each one of us.

I remember when I was planning for a Gospel Campaign in Manila which is a massive Catholic city. (Don't get me wrong: I work closely with many Catholic charismatics, but the religious spirits of Catholicism – and Protestantism – hate a move of the Holy Spirit) We had planned a big campaign in Luneta Plaza in Manila, where the Nation had just recently been dedicated to the Virgin Mary. I remember saying to Reinhard Bonnke the evangelist, that there was no way we were going to break through easily in that City. Catholicism was so strong, and Manila had seen an extraordinary supernatural move of some deceptive spirits: literally the week before we started, there were apparitions in the heavens with the "Virgin Mary" appearing, and there were incredible spiritual things happening which just confronted us. The priests had been warning the people of Manila: "don't go down to the campaign at Luneta Plaza!" So of course, they all came!

I remember saying to Reinhard Bonnke, "there is such a battle, we cannot just preach for six nights: we must extend the Crusade to 10 nights. Well, he preached his heart out every night, and every night we saw healing miracles. During those first five nights, miracles flowed powerfully with blind eyes opening, cripples walking, and the deaf hearing. There were extraordinary healing miracles - but nobody came to Christ! My Bible says that "the God of this world has blinded the minds of unbelievers" (2 Cor 4:4) and this blindness was so strong over the Catholic people that they could even witness the miracles on the stage, but their eyes were not being opened to the Gospel.

We had about a thousand intercessors behind the platform crying out to God every day for breakthrough. They were so frustrated that they could not break this demonic spirit that was holding Manila captive. However, on the fifth day, we heard such a massive shout behind the platform: it was as if something electric went straight through the whole crowd. The prayer and intercession team had broken through, and the power of God was released!

It was only a small crowd in Christ for All Nations experience - about 80000 - but something just exploded in revival power. Suddenly it was so obvious to us that everyone's eyes had been opened! Yes, there were miracles that night, but the most remarkable part of it was that when Reinhard gave the "altar call", about 80% of the crowd just seemed to run forward to give their lives to Jesus! The people of Manila had been so gripped and blinded by that religious spirit, so that they could not be transformed until their eyes were opened and they "saw" the Cross. They needed to "see" what Jesus had done for them, before they could run to the Cross. As I said, miracles were no problem, but salvation had been blocked by that spirit. Luke 16:31 says that "even if people rise from the dead they still won't be convinced." It's the same anywhere until we break through against the spirit of blindness. Since that moment, in Manila and the surrounding areas, there has been a rapid and marked growth in the number of people coming to Christ: revival was in the air, and God impacted the Philippines.

You can share stories like this with atheists, and often they will not believe in the power of God; they may even point to scientific reasons why miracles don't happen. I remember the night in Manila when my wife's legs were healed from being crippled in an accident in Zimbabwe a few years before. (we had been rescuing people from a car crash in front of our house when this happened;

she had one leg twisted 30 degrees and two and a half inches shorter.) Her legs were miraculously lengthened and straightened, but the doctors just said it must have been an unusual spasm and could not accept that it was a miracle! I'm sure that you can see by now, that you cannot fight that kind of secular thinking with human intellect. It is a wicked demonic spirit of unbelief, which grips people's minds. The people themselves are never our enemy, but our battle is with those wicked spiritual forces, which will not let them believe.

CHAPTER 9
TWO TYPES OF PEOPLE, AND TWO LAWS

As we start our journey in seeking to understand the Cross, we need to begin with the understanding that there are essentially two types of people: firstly, there are those who are being saved by God's direct intervention and God's direct action on the Cross. Secondly, there are those who are being deceived by the devil and who are going to hell. It is not a comfortable topic nowadays, but the reality is that some people are going to hell and are almost living in a foretaste of it before they die. Some people are just like lemmings charging into a Godless eternity and have no concept of what they are heading towards.

General Booth of the Salvation Army used to talk about the fact that he often felt he needed to hang his street evangelism teams for 20 minutes over the gateway down into hell before he sent them out. He said that they needed to be motivated by seeing for themselves just what people are being saved from. We must be gripped by this understanding of eternity, as often in our churches we don't have any understanding of hell. It's either sanitized or not preached about enough.

Just as there are two types of people, there are also two laws: there is firstly the law of "sin and death", which is gripping the bulk of humanity. Secondly there is the "law of the spirit of life in Christ Jesus". These are laws, and those laws work - because a law is a law. The law of sin and death will always drag people down: we will always be sucked down by the force of this law, and it doesn't matter what we do in terms of denying it or hiding it, sadly the law of sin will always pull us down. It's like the law of gravity which will always pull us down whether we believe in it or not!

In the natural there is however another law - and I know I'm stretching a point here - but there is the law of aerodynamics, which you discover when you actually make a choice to step onto a plane. Without having to do a thing and even without understanding how the law works, this law of aerodynamics will lift you up. Just by making a clear decision to take one simple step onto the plane - that changes everything! In the same way, spiritually, so many people just "hang around the airport" of church, thinking that this will somehow miraculously work; but if they won't "get on the plane" and get into Christ, they will never connect to the higher spiritual law. This is a higher law and it's "the law of the spirit of life" and it is only found *"in Christ Jesus"*.

As Christians, we have to recognize that people who are not "in Christ" will automatically be dragged down - sinners will end up sinning, and that is the human problem. We don't have to know how the cross works, just as you don't have to know how an airplane works! You just have to make a decision to get on the plane and trust it. Perhaps you might panic, "Oh dear! I've got to do something to stay up here. I can't trust this law of aerodynamics!": if you think that and rush to the plane door and open it so that you can somehow flap your arms – you are dead, along with many others! Sin kills not only you but often those around you. It's the exactly the same spiritually because many Christians think they can live a sinless life by themselves. They step into Christ and suddenly think: "I've got to do something! Help, I've just got to do something to earn this salvation", and they then get sucked down in works, works, and more works because they feel they have to try to prove something. They start falling and they get sucked down just like a non-Christian. So right at the outset, let's clearly establish in our minds about these two laws: the law of the spirit of life in Christ Jesus and the law a sin and death.

Now this seems so simple, but it is the underlying truth before we look at the Cross. The only thing that decides between these two groups is how they personally respond to the Cross. That may seem so unreal to many people, but it was really this truth that made me so mad at Christians and the Christian faith – which is why I asked the Colonel in charge of my Regiment to give me three years leave to go to Cambridge (with the hidden motivation of trying to disprove Christianity and religion.). I hated Christians because of this one thing: I hated the fact that they were talking about hell and damnation and sin - it just made no sense to me: it was what the Bible calls "foolishness".

So, as I shared earlier, I went to Cambridge University and I furiously read different books on different religions to try to package them, in order to prove that these religions were just mirror images of the societies that formed them. Once I'd completed this, I began to meet real Christians, who calmly said: "Great! It is wonderful that you've realized the emptiness of religion, even the "dead religion of Christianity". Now you can finally concentrate on the most wonderful thing – having a relationship with Jesus himself!"

This infuriated me and started me on my second short dissertation to try to disprove who Jesus was or claimed to be. This is how I got saved because the truth is, the more you focus on Jesus, the more you will be attracted to Him. So finally, after a lot of wrestling, I had that extraordinary encounter with God. I just knew that He was right there, because the holy presence of God flooded my houseboat and I knew that I was totally wrong. I need to confess something important to you now: the strange thing is that I didn't really get through with God for another 18 months – despite having a direct encounter with God!

The reason I'm sharing this is because I now live in Oxford ("the other place") and I am constantly meeting students who like me have made a mental assessment and have been intellectually fully converted. They feel in the same way that I did, that they know it all. They have their theology all sorted and lined up, and yet they really do not understand the "good news".

As I said, I knew the Bible better than all the Christians in my Christian Union, even before I was saved. However, it took me 18 months to be brought to the foot of the Cross - 18 months of trying to live the Christian life in my own strength, before I finally surrendered: it was months of helping alcoholics and drug addicts and trying to do it myself. Finally, I was so totally empty, and God chose this moment to speak to me through an Irish alcoholic: "To be sure, at least oi'm filled with a lot of "spirit", but you have absolutely nothing in yer!" I knew it was true! I had absolutely nothing of God's spirit in me, because it was all up in my mind. As I prayed, God just gave me an ultimatum: "How can you really know me? It's not by believing in me, because the devil believes, and he trembles. You will only really know me when you surrender everything into My hands: all the bad and all the good, surrender everything into My hands". At the foot of the Cross that night I got totally "born again" and filled with the Holy Spirit.

I know what it feels like to wrestle with this simple life-changing truth, as it does seem "foolishness" to so many people. What I found is that God deliberately "offends the minds of intellectuals - He offends human intellect, and human wisdom - to reveal what is truly in their heart". That is why I love being in Oxford: it is so offensive to some intellectuals and theologians, because I'm not a theologian - I just know God. Sadly, I've never been to Bible college, though I would have loved the privilege of having those years to really anchor my faith. God had other ways of imparting truth to me.

To religious people, the Cross is totally offensive - it just seems so wrong, and it doesn't make sense. To everybody else it is "total nonsense", but to us who simply believe, it is the very power of God and leads us into an experience of salvation. We read in Romans 1:16 "I am not ashamed of this Cross! I'm not ashamed of the Good News because it is the power of God for the salvation of everyone who believes". This message of the Cross needs to be so easy that anyone of any age and social background can understand it. It needs to be so simple that even a child can understand it.

We must not be intimidated by militant atheists and humanists who call our faith "nonsense". Psalm 2 says: *"Why does the enemy rage in vain against the Lord and against His anointed ones? Jesus sits enthroned in heaven and He laughs."* Yes, we will face some rough situations in the future, but we must never back away from the simplicity of the Cross. Our greatest enemy is our own strength and our own wisdom. God shames the wise and the strong by simply blessing the weak. He chooses the weak - he chooses the foolish people like us. He chooses us to "shame the wise", because He calls "the lowly and the despised." Many of us who never thought that God could ever care about us, have been overwhelmed by His outrageous grace. We suddenly found that everyone can qualify for His mercy and His grace! He does this so that nobody else can ever take the glory.

So often people will not come to the foot of the Cross. However, once we come to that place of absolute brokenness, something should happen! A declaration of the Cross should trigger something in us. When the Cross is preached it releases its power, because it is the preaching of the Cross of "Jesus Christ and Him crucified." When we preach this, something should happen in people's hearts, minds and spirits. Signs and wonders often begin to happen after the preaching of the Cross. The power of God begins to work in people's lives.

MAKE GOD'S LOVE GO VIRAL!

Before the Cross
Sold into slavery

"Jesus" on the Cross
Saved from the **slavery to Satan**

"Me" on the Cross
Saved from the **power of Sin**
ruling through my "old man"

"Self" on the Cross daily
Saved from the **power of Self**
ruling through my "flesh"

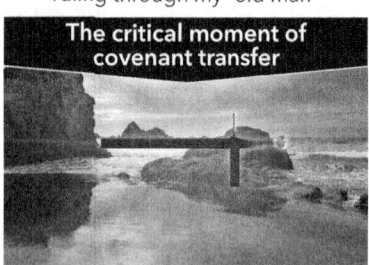

The critical moment of covenant transfer

"The world" on the Cross
Cross over point from minus to plus

Covenanted to Christ
Cross over from **Satan into "Sonship"**

Covenanted to His body
Cross over from **Self into "Service"**

Covenanted back into the world to seek and save the lost
Cross over from **Sin into "Suffering"**

CHAPTER 10

THE SEVEN STAGES OF THE CROSS

Remember what Paul writes to the Corinthian Church which was in a serious mess at the time: "For Christ didn't send me to baptize, but to preach the Gospel - not with words of human wisdom lest *the Cross of Christ be emptied of its power. For the message of the Cross is foolishness to those who are perishing but to us who are being saved, it is the power of God."* (1 Cor 1:17-18) He goes on to say: "For I resolved to know nothing while I was with you, except Jesus Christ and Him crucified. I came to you in weakness and fear and with much trembling. My message and my preaching were not with wise and persuasive words but with *a demonstration of the Spirit's power, so that your faith may not rest on men's wisdom but on God's power."* (1 Cor 2: 2-5)

Please forgive me but my military background will come through much of my illustration. There are many different metaphors and illustrations on the Cross because it is such a central feature of our Christian faith. Some people think of the Cross as going "from minus to plus." That was the title of Reinhard Bonnke's booklet that went out many years ago to millions of homes. This indicated that moment when God changed all of human history, turning our human "minus" into God's mighty "plus", as Jesus carried our misery, sin, sickness, hatred, loneliness, and isolation and gave us instead God's love, forgiveness, healing, freedom and connectedness with God. Other people see it as "the connection from heaven to earth" - heaven finally being able to connect to earth, with God embracing the whole of humanity.

My understanding of the Cross is this: the Cross of Christ's sacrifice being turned around by God to become the sword of the Lord – the sword of God's victory. This is what we will explain carefully through these pages. We are going to take a journey through the seven stages of the cross; each stage turns the Cross until it is completely the other way around, and it becomes this mighty sword of the Lord. (See the illustrations) I do need to emphasize that we are talking in the spiritual world, as we all know how damaging it was to the Gospel when the Crusaders failed to understand that "people are never our enemy." As Paul wrote to the Ephesian church, now in South Turkey, we must realize that we only fight spirits in the spiritual realm. By misunderstanding this, the Crusaders turned the Cross into physical swords 900 years ago and brought carnage and devastation from France all the way through to Jerusalem. That tragic misrepresentation of the Bible left a wound that Islam still carries today and is one of the primary reasons for its total mistrust of the West.

We are going to go on a journey, which in some ways will reflect the journey that the Israelites took when they broke free of the control and domination of the Egyptians, as they crossed out of Egypt over the Red Sea; it will also reflect their continuing journey through the wilderness until they finally crossed over the Jordan into their inheritance and promised land. This spiritually reflects our journey out of the control and domination of Sin and Satan's grip in our lives, and then our journey into all the fullness and promises of God: the first stages are crossing out of the negative, and the second stages are *crossing into* the positive.

> » Our journey is starting in that era of history before the Cross; it starts in the heart of God, knowing that His precious creation of mankind had been sold into slavery to Satan when Adam sinned in the garden of Eden. This is the dark period of history when there was no light and no breakthrough.

- » But then came the *first stage* of the cross when we see *"Jesus on the Cross."* This triumphant, earth-changing moment is when we are *saved from slavery to Satan*, and we cross out from Satan's dominion and power.

- » The *second stage* of the Cross, is when *"little old me"* is placed on the Cross by faith, and I am *saved from the power of Sin* ruling through my "old man." You can see in the diagram how we are beginning to "get a handle on the Cross." Here we cross out from the power and dominion of Sin in our lives.

- » The *third stage* of the cross is *my flesh being placed on the Cross - daily!* This is when we are *saved from the power of Self* - all that self-centredness and selfishness, which rules me through my flesh. Here we cross out from the power and dominion of "my flesh" - but this a daily life-long walk of faith.

- » This takes us onto the *fourth stage* of the Cross which is really the critical moment where many people get stuck. It is the critical moment of covenant transfer when we finally place *the world on the Cross*. This is the crossover point from "minus to plus", when we *cross over into our "promised land" of all that Jesus won for us;* sadly some people never cross over out from the subtle influence and control of worldly thinking.

- » On the other side of the Cross as it begins to turn over to become a sword, we cross over into the fact that we are now covenanted to Christ. In the *fifth stage* of the Cross, we *"cross over from Satan into Sonship"*.

- » Then the *sixth stage* of the cross is where we come into a covenant with His Body of the Church, and we *"cross over from Self into Service"*.

- » And finally, in the *seventh stage* of the Cross we are covenanted back into the world just like Christ, to seek and save the lost; this is where we *"cross over from Sin into Sacrifice and suffering"* which is when God's love finally goes viral through our lives! This is the progression in our journey of activating every aspect of the Cross. So, fasten your seat belts as we start on this remarkable journey!

CHAPTER 11

OUR SLAVERY TO THE DEVIL IS BROKEN

BEFORE THE CROSS
Sold into Slavery

First let's look at the state of the world before the Cross. All of mankind was sold into slavery when Adam and Eve disobeyed God and they became the slaves of Satan, subjected to the curse of sin, sickness and poverty. In ancient times there was an understanding when somebody was sold into slavery: a scroll was written out designating two things: firstly, the name of their nearest "kinsman redeemer", and secondly the price that it would cost them to buy that slave back from slavery. ("Redeem" or "redemption" simply means "paying the price to buy back from slavery") So here, in the spirit realm, it was as if a scroll had been written specifying the terms of the redemption of mankind. We see this in Revelation 5 when we hear that heart cry of humanity, "Who is worthy to open the scroll, and who can redeem mankind back from slavery to the devil?" They look everywhere to find somebody who could redeem mankind, but nobody comes forward.

What we see in Revelation 5, is that Jesus suddenly appears as the "kinsman redeemer": He is the only one who could legally buy us back and "redeem" us from Satan's grip of ownership and control. It shows this in Hebrews 10:7, when we see Jesus coming to God the Father and saying: "Here I am: I know that it's my name that's written in that scroll. I am the only legal "kinsman redeemer" for mankind. Right now, I've come to do your will. I know what it's going to cost, but I also know that the Lamb has been slain since the foundation of the world. I am that Lamb and I have come to do your will."

Suddenly Jesus appears as the Lamb who was slain, the Lion from the tribe of Judah, the root of David. The whole cry of humanity changes, and we hear them shouting out: "You are worthy! You are worthy to take the scroll and open its seals! - Jesus you're the only one who can legally open up the scroll of the slavery of mankind and redeem mankind, because you were slain as the Lamb of God, and with your blood you have purchased men for God from every tribe, language, people and nation!" His blood purchased every man, woman, and child that exists or will ever exist – He has bought us. You and I already belong to Him!

"JESUS" ON THE CROSS
Saved from the **Slavery to Satan**

As we begin to look at the first stage of the Cross, we must get this sealed into our spirit: Jesus has broken that slavery to Satan through His death on the Cross. On the Cross, He cried out "It is finished!": this meant, "I have paid this redemption price in absolute fullness. There is nothing left to be paid. I have paid this debt in full!" What a shout! He knew it was done, and He had purchased with His blood every man, woman, and every child. And that's why we are no longer slaves to sin, sickness and poverty; nor do we have the fruit of it in our lives which can cause intense shame to hang over believers for years. We are not only forgiven, we are also washed clean and healed. We no longer have to submit to shame or regret, or the pain of sin or sickness or to the curse of poverty or to any of the rubbish that Satan wants to inflict on us. Jesus broke it, He paid for it, and this is the "good news" - but it does need a personal response from us and it needs acceptance.

However, every slave still has a choice: we must see that slaves in those days could actually choose not to be set free. They could be taken to the door posts and have a nail hammered through their ear lobe - that's pretty gruesome - but a slave had this choice which would then bind them eternally to their master. We are free to choose in the same way whether we accept the freedom through Jesus or we remain enslaved by the devil. Remarkably many still choose to reject God's offer of freedom. Millions in fact still choose to stay enslaved: even though their freedom is paid for, they still choose to stay as slaves of the devil.

Colossians 2:15 says that "Jesus totally disarmed all the powers and all the authorities, and He made a public spectacle of them triumphing over them by the Cross". On the Cross it was "a once and for all" moment - the total defeat of every principality and every demonic power. Jesus broke the grip of Satan's hold over each one of us. We must realize this in our spirits - *the devil has no legal right to hold people in slavery unless they choose to reject that offer of redemption.*

It says in John 16:11 that "when the Holy Spirit comes, He will convince us of certain things": one major thing is that He will convince us in regard to the devil's status after the event of the Cross: he has already been sentenced because the "prince of this world now stands condemned." We need to realize that the sentence against the devil has already been passed *but the judgment has not yet happened.* Often we hear people complaining: "God, why can't you just close down the devil? Why can't you just close the books and judge the devil and stop all this mess?" The answer is that God's Kingdom has a "righteous government" which He instituted in the universe, and he has to keep to his own righteous government. You see, although the devil has been sentenced, the judgment has not been carried out yet. The righteous government, which God put in place in His Kingdom, decrees that if

He brings down the hammer of judgement against the devil, then all other judgments must happen *at the same time*. This means that God would also have to bring every man, woman, and child to judgment at the same time.

So we are living right now in this "time of grace", when God still has to allow the enemy to have room to move, because He also wants to give all of humanity the chance to respond to His grace. However, there will come a day when we are all brought to judgment and the devil will also be brought to judgment at that time. These are the final days of God's grace. We must understand that the devil has been sentenced already in the court of heaven, but the judgment will come in the future. The glorious truth however, for those of us that have responded, is that our slavery to the devil is totally broken! *At this first stage of the Cross, we see Jesus on the Cross, which saves us from slavery to Satan*. It totally deals with every single claim that Satan has over us, and the demonic control of sin, sickness and poverty in our lives.

What we have seen here is fantastic, but it is only half of the picture. Yes, it removes all the negative, but then there is the positive aspect of God's longing to be restored into intimacy with us. God's passion and longing is still to be "walking in the garden" with us again. The heart cry of Father God is still "Where are you?" He doesn't just want to set us free, He wants to be bonded in relationship with us eternally and restore to us the invisible realm of His Kingdom. How then does He restore us to live in His presence with Him?

CHAPTER 12

OUR INTIMACY WITH OUR FATHER IS RESTORED

It is at this point in our study and reflections that we need to recognize our own spiritual state. It says about us in Eph 2:1-3, "And his fullness fills you, even though you were once like corpses, dead in your sins and offenses. It wasn't that long ago that you lived in the religion, customs, and values of this world, obeying the dark ruler of the earthly realm who fills the atmosphere with his authority, and works diligently in the hearts of those who are disobedient to the truth of God. The corruption that was in us from birth was expressed through the deeds and desires of our self-life. We lived by whatever natural cravings and thoughts our minds dictated, living as rebellious children subject to God's wrath like everyone else."

We must understand that we were "objects of God's wrath." We don't preach about this much, but we must try to feel our way into trying to understand what is going on in God's heart, which creates this blazing anger. I'm a parent and I'm sure many of us parents can understand a little bit about this "wrath". You see, as parents we also have two sides to our character. We do have that blazing anger against disobedience when we know that there is something negative that is gripping our kids; but at the same time, we also have an absolute passionate love for our kids.

These are the two different faces of a parent: hatred of the disobedience, and yet love for our child. Sadly, our children sometimes only see the face of blazing anger, with little demonstration of that love. We must show them both sides otherwise we will damage them. What I want you to see is that God is our parent too. He has both faces. He shows the face of His "wrath" or blazing anger because He hates sin. The moral part of God is outraged at what sin does to His children; but He also has a passion for us, loves us and longs for us. So here we have the face of hatred of sin and rebellion, but also the face of mercy and love.

Our sin of independence and disobedience creates a massive reaction in God's heart. I often used to think that Adam's sin was in taking that apple. No! Adam's sin was essentially that he wanted to live in independence from God - he wanted to "do his own thing." Adam's prime sin is independence. Taking the apple was the fruit of that sin. His sin was that he wanted to be independent, and live independently from God, and it's that root that has to be dealt with. We have to face up to that root in us and bring that to the Cross. Yes, God loves us, but he's outraged at what He sees developing inside us: our rebellion and our independence is really offensive to Him. We need a revelation of how much our sin wounds Him and how much it cost Him to pay the penalty for it. We read in 1 John 2:2 that "Jesus became the atoning sacrifice for our sins, not only for ourselves but also for the sins of the whole world."

For many of us in this modern society, the concept of the "blood" doesn't compute with our culture; but back in those days and in many tribal cultures today, it was natural to understand that "blood" meant "life". So in Lev 17:11 God talks about how "the life of the creature is in the blood. I've given it to you to make atonement for yourself on the altar." It is the blood that makes atonement for one's life. So Father God knew and Jesus knew, what it was going to cost Him. His own blood had to be poured out to atone for all of our sins. It cost him everything, because He had to pour out all of His blood.

If you are in church long enough, you will hear the theological word "propitiate". I used to hate that word "propitiate" until I realized what it meant: it means that the blood of Jesus is more than adequate to fully satisfy the righteous government of God against sin. We tend to talk about "expiation" - just wiping sin out; but this is impossible in the righteous government of God, as it decrees that sin has a penalty of death, and someone must pay. That would be the equivalent of a High Court judge just saying: "I know this murder carries the penalty of death, but I've decided to just set you free." There would be an outrage from those who have been affected: murder has a penalty. In the same way, sin has a penalty – death; remember "the wages of sin is death". Jesus chose to pay the penalty for all of our sin.

Some might think: "Isn't God such a loving God. Won't He just overlook it?" No! He had to pay for it: this is so important to grasp: He was humiliated; He was stripped bare; He was flogged; He was lacerated; if you've seen "the Passion" film, the way Jesus was treated was gruesome. We must personally realize "this is what it took to deliver me from all of my sin." He was stripped naked and flogged, He had nails put in his hands and feet on that Cross. He was absolutely brutalized and was left hanging there in agony for me and for you. When the full realization of the horror of His crucifixion hits us, something profound happens inside us. When we fully understand the cost He paid, we will hopefully stop messing around with sin, as we realize that the Cross really did cost Jesus everything!

What I want to convey here is that our "cheap grace" is not "good news". Let's not be guilty of offering "cheap grace" to people. We must not be believers who talk all the time about the love of God, but don't balance the message with the foundational truth that God is also holy! This error is at the root of the movement to embrace an unbiblical view on the whole area of sexuality and gender issues. It doesn't set people free. Perhaps they might have a little "touch of the Spirit" but often it doesn't set them free. I've watched too many Christians being touched by the Spirit but then realizing they are still not free.

To some extent, it is correct when preachers say: "I know you're in a mess. Come on, come to Jesus and He'll clean you up, and He'll heal you." Yes, of course that is His heart and He does all of that; but first each one of us needs to face the holiness of our Father God, and His absolute outrage at our rebellion and our independence. There is this missing word of "repentance" which is so vital. I believe that we are totally set free when we come in brokenness and repentance to Him. We need to say, "Father, I'm so, so sorry! I've seen it now, and I'm going to give up all my independence and my rebellion." Suddenly, we feel those chains broken and we begin to get free, because freedom starts by taking responsibility, and repenting.

Yes, God is going to forgive us, but He needs us to see our sin as He sees it and then begin to hate it. "God I was wrong! God I'm so sorry!" Often we hate those two words - saying "I was wrong" and "I am so sorry". It is so helpful though in counselling to actually ask people to confess "I was wrong", and then to say to other people "I am so sorry". Those two words are powerful! They do so much in the restoration of trust and relationship.

We've seen that God poured out of all His righteous anger against the sin of mankind, but we've also seen how Jesus fulfilled and satisfied the righteous government of the universe, in choosing to lay His life down to pay for all our sins. Since the penalty for our sins could not be overlooked, Jesus took it all. We know the scripture of Isaiah 53 so well, that Jesus "was despised and rejected by men, a man of deep sorrows who was no stranger to suffering and grief. We hid our faces from him in disgust and considered him a nobody, not worthy of respect. Yet he was the one who carried our sicknesses and endured the torment of our sufferings. We viewed him as one who was being punished for something he himself had done, as one who was struck down by God and brought low. But it was because of our rebellious deeds that he was pierced and because of our sins that he was crushed. He endured the punishment that made us completely whole, and in his wounding, we found our healing. Like wayward sheep, we have all wandered astray. Each of us has turned from God's paths and chosen our own way; even so, God laid the guilt of our every sin upon Him."

Wow! The power of those words! You see, he was my substitute. He was your substitute. He was the scapegoat who took all of our sin. You may remember the story of the scapegoat in the Old Testament: how the priest made people lay their hands on the scapegoat and impart all their sin onto that scapegoat and then the priest chased it off into the wilderness. Jesus was the lamb that was slain; He was the scapegoat; He was the substitute for each one of us. He took it all on himself. He knew he had to fulfil the righteous government of God.

I know I'm labouring this again and again, but we must see that this is all about the righteous government of God, because God cannot break His own laws. The Bible says in 2 Cor 5: 21 that He actually "became sin for us. God made Him who had no sin to be sin for us so that in Him we might become the righteous of God". He actually became sin! Can you imagine it? All of that filth and that "yuck" - all the filth of the holocaust, the paedophilia, the murder, the adultery, the sexual impurity - everything! Every last drop was poured onto Jesus. He took it all, and He took my curse so that I could be blessed. (Gal 3).

I trust by now that you are definitely "on the plane" - fully committed and trusting in Jesus. I say again, that you do not need to fully understand all the technicalities of how the Cross works, or how by stepping into Christ by faith you will be lifted up from the law of sin and death; you just need to trust Him and step by faith into Him, as if you were stepping onto a plane. If you haven't done this already, before we move on, please settle this with Jesus: He's looking for an unconditional surrender of your life into His hands, and a decision of faith to receive all of His life and love into your life.

We then need to decide to stay in Him and in His Word. So, as we close this chapter, let's take time to respond and just soak in these amazing words that Paul wrote to the people in Colossians 1: "Even though you were once distant from God, living in the shadows of your evil thoughts and actions, He reconnected you back to Himself. He released his supernatural peace to you through the sacrifice of His own body as the sin-payment on your behalf so that you would dwell in His presence. And now there is nothing between you and Father God, for He sees you as holy, flawless, and restored, if indeed you continue to advance in faith, assured of a firm foundation to grow upon. Never be shaken from the hope of the gospel you have believed in: this is the glorious news I preach all over the world." (Col 1:21-23 TPT)

Colossians 2 then says that "through our union with Jesus we have experienced a circumcision of heart. All of the guilt and power of sin has been cut away and is now extinct because of what Christ, the anointed one, has accomplished for us. For we've been buried with Him into His death. Our "baptism into death" also means that we were raised with Him when we believed in God's resurrection power, the same power that raised Him from death's realm. This "realm of death" describes our former state, for we were held in sin's grasp. But now, we've been resurrected out of that "realm of death" never to return, for we are forever alive and forgiven of all our sins!

He cancelled out every legal violation we had on our record and the old arrest warrant that stood to indict us. He erased it all—our sins, our stained soul—he deleted it all and they cannot be retrieved! Everything we once were in Adam has been placed onto his Cross and nailed permanently there as a public display of cancellation. Then Jesus made a public spectacle of all the powers and principalities of darkness, stripping away from them every weapon and all their spiritual authority and power to accuse us: *by the power of the Cross, Jesus led them around as prisoners in a procession of triumph.* He was not their prisoner; they were his!" (Col 2:11-15 TPT)

This is the face we know so well as Christians: Jesus on the Cross. But is it more than a theology to you? It surely has to be more than that! Are you convinced that Jesus died for you – and for me? Are you convinced that we no longer have to be slaves to the devil? We no longer have to be slaves to sin, or slaves to sickness, to the curses over our lives, to poverty, or to any other negative demonic assignments. The devil has no legal right to hold us. Today, let's make a stand, and make a clear decision: "No! The devil has no legal right over my life. I'm on my way out: I'm going to walk out of the devil's control!"

I know that things will not all change overnight. It is a journey, but we must choose to be free from slavery, and choose to be free from regret, fear, guilt and shame. Let's choose to be free of sin, sickness, the curse and, far more than that, let's choose to be reconciled to a holy God. He has set us free, but He also wants us to be totally reconciled to Him and to truly know that oneness with Him. Remember, we must face up to the wrath of God, facing up to our rebellion and our independence. The key to the revivals that have happened in history was that 90% of their preaching was affirming God's law, because people are by nature in rebellion and independence against God. Then when people finally recognized they needed saving from hell, then the grace of God was preached.

With the "New Cross", we tend to do it the other way around, 90% grace and love and very little about God's law. Perhaps we should change the way we preach, because surely people need to know there is a "moral law." It's not relative - it is black and white. The Bible is very clear: Jesus came to make it very clear that we need to be saved from sin. He makes it very clear, that His direct action on the Cross is saving me from an eternity in hell. People need to recognize that sin has a cost. It has a price, but Jesus has taken it all! What a God! What a Saviour!

CHAPTER 13

OUR INHERITANCE IS GUARANTEED

Let's look closely at Jesus as He steps into the water at the age of 30. He has lived a faultless life and now at 30, the Jewish legal age of inheritance, Jesus knows that something remarkable is about to happen. At 30, every son and heir is displayed before all the relatives and friends, and the father shouts out "This is my beloved son and heir, and I am so pleased with him!" From that moment, all the father's estate, property, power and authority are legally passed over to his son, and the father retires into the family.

The scene is set: this D-Day has been planned and dreamed of for an eternity. Father God has sent John the Baptist on ahead to tell everyone about the coming return and invasion of His Kingdom. John tells everyone to prepare their hearts, because someone is coming who is the "Lamb of God" who will take away all the sins of all humanity. He tells them that the return of the Kingdom of God is imminent. John doesn't know that the clock is ticking, but Jesus does: Jesus is well aware that He is approaching the age of 30, and he also knows that His true father is not the carpenter, but the Lord God Almighty, Creator of heaven and earth. He is not simply dreaming of inheriting Joseph's business; He knows He is about to step into a transfer of power and authority of cosmic proportions.

Jesus marches down to the Jordan to meet John, knowing that something is about to explode. He sinks under the water, symbolically bringing all of his humanity into that watery grave, then He shoots up out of the water and the Holy Spirit comes upon Him.

The cry of His Father is heard! "This is my beloved Son and heir, and I am so pleased with him!" D-Day has arrived, and the unstoppable force of the Kingdom of God is legally transferred onto Jesus, so that He can now break through the lines of the enemy, and totally break his control and ownership of mankind.

The alarm bells are ringing wildly in hell, because suddenly a man is standing there on earth, for the first time in history since mankind was enslaved in Eden, and He now has all the legal power and authority in heaven and earth on His shoulders! Satan throws everything he can muster at Jesus, just to make Him doubt for one moment what has just happened and feel that this is all a dream; but no, nothing can shake the resolve in Jesus as the Holy Spirit takes Him into the wilderness for a showdown with the devil.

Jesus wrestles in his spirit but knows that the Holy Spirit is filling Him daily despite his lack of food for 40 days. Day after day he is taunted by demons trying to shake his total faith, confidence and belief that He is legally the son and heir with the right to all power and authority. Daily He raises His one and only weapon – the sword of His Word: "It is written! It is written! It is written!" After 40 days, the battle in the wilderness is won! He was taken into this wilderness time having been filled by the Holy Spirit, but now He comes out in the power and authority of the Son of God, with a mandate to proclaim the invasion of a new Kingdom back on earth. Everywhere he goes, he is proclaiming that the Kingdom of God has broken through the time warp and it is now available to whosoever would simply come to Him, believe, and receive.

I have tried to describe this scene graphically, because each one of us who chooses to pursue the Kingdom of God in our lives, must walk this walk. So many enthusiastically come to Jesus, receive Father's forgiveness and restoration and then ask to be filled with the Holy Spirit. Whoever asks receives – there is no question about that. However, there is a distinct difference between knowing the fullness of the Spirit and knowing His power and authority. Each one of us must, in a similar way to Jesus, fight the battle for faith in the wilderness, holding onto our child-like faith that we are called to be carriers and executors of this invisible realm of the Kingdom, rescuing the lost, healing the sick, raising the dead, and casting out demons.

Our only weapon will be the weapon Jesus wielded - the Word - and our only cry has to be "No! I'm a believer! I have the legal right to this sonship and authority by faith. This is what is written – Satan, back off!" We too will come out of those wilderness experiences in the power and authority of the Kingdom. Remember what Jesus said: "Anyone who has faith in me will do what I have been doing, and they will do even greater things than these, because I am going to the Father. (John 14:12)

So Jesus walks out of the wilderness utterly triumphant, and instantly draws a crowd - no advertising, and no multi-media promotion. He immediately demonstrates the Kingdom; first with signs and wonders and miracles and then He gives some explanation. He unpacks this new Kingdom, not to the crowd however, but to His disciples. He is training His first Kingdom leaders. He tells them that it's about heart surrender not outward observance, totally contrary to worldly thinking – the upside-down Kingdom. He demonstrates the contrast between human intellect, and the revelation knowledge of the Kingdom. Peter and John were just "unlearned and ignorant men" but they were soon operating in the same power and authority of the Kingdom. The invasion of the Kingdom of God had found a beachhead. The scene was now set for generations in the future to invade the kingdoms of darkness and set billions free from the tyranny of darkness! Come on, God!

CHAPTER 14

FREE AT LAST FROM MY EGO-SELF AND "LITTLE OLD ME"!

"ME" ON THE CROSS
Saved from the **power of Sin** ruling through my "old man"

Let's settle into this subject and listen to old apostle Paul as he's talking to those in Rome. "What a terrible thought! We have died to sin once and for all, as a dead man passes away from this life. So how could we live under sin's rule a moment longer? Or have you forgotten that all of us who were immersed into union with Jesus, the Anointed One, were immersed into union with His death? Sharing in His death by our baptism means that we were co-buried and entombed with Him, so that when the Father's glory raised Christ from the dead, we were also raised with Him. We have been co-resurrected with Him so that we could be empowered to walk in the freshness of new life. For since we are permanently grafted into Him to experience a death like his, then we are permanently grafted into Him to experience a resurrection like His and the new life that it imparts.

Could it be any clearer that our former identity is now and forever deprived of its power? For we were co-crucified with him to dismantle the stronghold of sin within us, so that we would not continue to live one moment longer submitted to sin's power. Obviously, a dead person is incapable of sinning. And if we were co-crucified with the Anointed One, we know that we will also share in the fullness of his life. And we know that since the Anointed One has been raised from the dead to die no more, his resurrection life has vanquished death and its power over Him is finished. For by His sacrifice He died to sin's power once and for all, but He now lives continuously for the Father's pleasure. So let it be the same way with you! Since you are now joined with Him, you must continually view yourselves as dead and unresponsive to sin's appeal while living daily for God's pleasure in union with Jesus, the Anointed One. Sin is a dethroned monarch; so you must no longer give it an opportunity to rule over your life, controlling how you live and compelling you to obey its desires and cravings. So then, refuse to answer its call to surrender your body as a tool for wickedness. Instead, passionately answer God's call to keep yielding your body to Him as one who has now experienced resurrection life! You live now for His pleasure, ready to be used for His noble purpose. Remember this: sin will not conquer you, for God already has! You are not governed by law but governed by the reign of the grace of God." (Rom 6: 2-14 TPT)

There is no clearer way to start this chapter than to listen to these amazing words which Paul writes to the Church in Rome. Wow! What a word from heaven! In the first stage of the Cross we have seen "Jesus on the Cross". Stage one of the Cross deals very much with the fruit of what has happened in the Fall. This negative fruit obviously was our slavery to Satan, but we realized that our separation from God was also a result of the Fall. Stage one breaks that slavery but also reconnects us to intimacy with God. The redemption price has been paid in full! Jesus shouts out on the Cross: "It is finished! The debt has been totally paid!"

Sadly, the Christian reality is that many people camp at the first stage of the Cross for their entire lives, because they are never told there is more. This was my reality when I first came to Christ. We know we are forgiven but we still struggle with sin and we live in frustration: we live lives of defeat. Because of this reality, too many new believers then hide themselves behind facades of religion and they just keep on going around and around in religious circles – just as the Children of Israel walked around and around the wilderness. They never come into the fullness of their inheritance. As a pastor I am constantly counselling people who say "I know I'm saved, but I'm just not free. I know I have these strongholds in my life and the enemy mocks me. I just cannot break these strongholds."

After I was saved during the revival in Cambridge university, I saw many wonderful students coming to the Lord from lots of different backgrounds. I found it so sad however to watch some of them slowly beginning to step back into the shadows. This really puzzled me because I'd been saved in the white heat of an encounter with God - it was just amazing. But I watched people fade away. One of my close friends slowly slipped back because he could not get over his sexuality. He had a problem with his sexual identity and he couldn't believe that God could take that label from him. Other people had problems with their lust, and their thought life; others with relationships, or just simply with loneliness, or their past.

So, I watched these people who had been saved in the white heat of a real revival, where we had hundreds of people in the

Bible studies on a Friday night. There were prayer meetings every morning but slowly, even in that atmosphere, I watched people slipping back into the shadows. It really hurt me. I kept saying: "Why, God? Why? What is the problem?". Every one of them knew they were saved, but they also knew that were not free - and what's worse - they had no faith that they could ever be free.

Now when I came to Christ, nobody ever told me that there was more to the Cross than Jesus on the Cross. Nobody ever told me that there was a progression and a journey. So I lived in defeat myself; but I had read again and again in my Bible that God said through Paul to the Church in Rome that "Sin shall not be your master!"(Rom 6:14). I just had to believe that. If I didn't believe that, then there was no point in going on. I had to believe that there is something in God and in his Cross that can break the power of sin in my life.

So, what is this pivotal key for victory in the Christian life? This is the million-dollar question! Romans 6 holds the pivotal key for victory over sin: as I've said before, Jesus didn't die just to *improve* us - He came to remove us. He had to destroy that "little old me" because once he'd dispensed with this part of me, then His new creation could come alive in my life. The key is that because He died, by faith I died too. His Cross becomes my Cross, and so we now come on our journey to the *second stage of the Cross* which is *"little old me"- my self-life - on the Cross*. It took me ages before I finally recognized that I had to go to the Cross. Yes, Jesus on the Cross is fantastic, but once "little old me" (my ego and self-life) is on the Cross with Him, I know deep in my spirit that *I am saved from the power of sin and shame ruling through my "old man" or "old self"*.

This stage of the journey deals with what we call "the three-fold root of the "old Man"". Let me describe it, because this is three separate roots. First of all, it is the root of Adam's sin. Remember that we are all part of Adam's race, so I'm definitely going to be tainted with Adam's sin. There is going to be something that is inherited and comes into me simply because I'm a human being. That is the first thing, but the second thing is that I am also brought up in a family and in an environment: I'm shaped by that. I'm shaped by my parents, my school and my environment. So, the first two things that shape me are the Adamic sin, and my personal environment. The third thing however is all my personal choices: if I choose to sin and live in independence or rebellion – all these choices shape me.

These are the three roots of the "old man": our hereditary past, our parental and educational past, and finally our personal past and history. These roots are all called together "the old man" or "the old self". What you and I need to appropriate, is that when we place ourselves on the Cross by faith, all that "old man" has been destroyed on the Cross with Jesus! We have to believe that on the Cross that part of the old me - "my old man" - was rendered powerless. The problem is that I have to not only believe all this, but also have to take it into my life by faith: I have to know it and receive it "by revelation."

You see the full sin of Adam's race was poured onto Jesus. It was unbelievable filth! He took it all – every one of the hereditary, parental, educational, and personal roots. He became sin and broke the power of each of these roots which have controlled me. Can you imagine all of that sin just being poured into Him? It's almost impossible to conceive of that volume of sin! All that sin was placed on Him. No wonder in the garden he said "Father, if it's possible, let this cup pass from me." He knew what He was about to experience: the sinless, stainless, spotless Lamb of God was going to have to drink all this to the full. He became sin, taking on such filth for me!

For you and I, this second stage of the Cross renders powerless all of these roots in my "old man". Not only does it destroy those roots, but it also destroys the domination of "little old me". If I choose to believe that I am on the Cross with Jesus, then "my old man" is on the Cross too. Can you see that I no longer have to be rooted back into my past life? This is such freedom, and it is simply activated by faith: if I believe it then I begin to walk into it; if I don't believe it, I just stay in my shadow. God sees so many people walking back into their shadows of fear and unbelief, because they will not believe. They walk away from the Cross into their shadow, because they have not fixed their eyes on Jesus, and walked into His light. My Bible says that if we fix our eyes on Jesus and what He's done on the Cross, we can walk out of our past. But so many people walk back into their shadows and they keep on rehearsing areas of guilt, pain and shame, and remembering things of the past.

Whatever you focus on, will end up controlling you; whatever you fix your eyes on, will rule you. We must discipline the way we think and stop looking at the past. Cut yourself off from it and start fixing your eyes on Jesus. The Bible says that "as we behold Him we are being transformed from glory into glory." It's the "beholding Him" that changes us. This is a mystery, but as a Pastor I constantly witness too many Christians going around and around, rehearsing their past wounds, together with their past hurts. Everybody has been through "stuff!" Listen, once we put ourselves on the Cross by faith, that "old man" is rendered powerless: it can no longer hold us now, when we activate our faith. This is where I die, and my life ends, and I no longer have to struggle to conquer sin.

I'm sure you've tried to conquer sin, because we all do it. When I was saved, I thought "now I have to live a good life". I did try and do good things, but very soon I realized that it's humanly impossible to live a perfect Christian life. Nobody ever told me that. We cannot humanly defeat sin; we have to live daily by the Spirit, trusting in Him. That is why most mornings at home, I will drop to my knees on the carpet, and "break bread" alone with God and say "Father, I can't do this without you. I need you! I need your Spirit: I'm utterly dependent on your strength. I can't do anything without you!"

Before this, I was such a self-made man: I come from a family line of Generals, Admirals and five generations of military officers and this had developed such a wrong self-confidence and pride. I was so arrogant thinking that I could do it. My wife Rachel even keeps a photograph of me from those days, to remind me of what I looked like: it shows me standing in my uniform in a very "posh" place with my elbow on the mantelpiece, almost looking down on the world! God really had to deliver me from this and break that arrogance and pride which made me think that I could live the Christian life with my own effort- I could succeed and could do great things for God! It was all about me! I remember when I left Cambridge and went back to my regiment in Germany, I began to recognize that there was something wrong, because God seemed a million miles away. Perhaps you know too what it feels like when God has issues with you!

I used to pray in the army chapel almost every night and used to cry out to God, because I was so desperate for His presence, since there were no other Christians in the Regiment. One evening I saw that a dove had come into the church; each time I tried to catch this dove and throw it out of the church, it just flapped away. It flew up and hit the rafters and then landed exhausted somewhere else. Every time I tried to catch it and put my hands on it - off it flew. It took seven days before it finally got the message: it could not set itself free and it lay there panting on the floor. As I put my hands around it and took it to the door to release it, God spoke so clearly to me! "That is exactly what you're like! That's what you are doing to me - you will not let me put My hands on you! Every time I try to put My hands on you, you flap away and say: "I can do it! I can do it!" Then you hit so many problems that you realize you're trapped and can't get free. Just admit that you can't do it. When will you get the message? You have to die to your "self"!"

That proud, arrogant "little me" inside me at that time, just had to go to the Cross! God sometimes needs to get in our face; He wouldn't let me worm my way out of this: I just had to get out of the driving seat, because I was so much in control - so much a self-made man. You know, at times we all think that we can do it ourselves, but this part of us has to be broken. We must come to that place where we recognize "I can do nothing without you! God, I need your Spirit and your grace!" This is the attitude we need to live with daily. Now, having embraced "brokenness", life and grace is able to flow daily. My "old man" no longer dominates me and destroys my life: I am free at last from my unbroken ego - that dominating, controlling "little old me!"

CHAPTER 15

SPIRITUAL LESSONS FROM MARRIAGE AND BAPTISM

Over the years I have found that the key to this "life of salvation" is very similar to the key to having a successful marriage, because selfishness is also the number one killer within marriage. The key is that "little me" has to die. The trouble is that "little me" doesn't like dying. Let me illustrate this with part of the wedding ceremony which I often encourage when I preside over a wedding - I learnt this from Portugal. After the wedding vows, both mothers come forward having each lit a candle; they present these candles to the bride and groom who then walk up to the altar carrying their candle and then together they light a big brand-new candle. Now comes the important part: at the same moment, they then step back and blow out the candle they are carrying. This is so symbolic! The selfish "little me" in both the bride and groom is blown out and a "new creation" is formed!

You see, the trouble with most of our failing marriages, is that most of us don't want to blow our candle out. We feel: "It's all about me and my rights! You need to look after me!" However, if we live for each other and try to "out-serve" each other, marriage can be heaven. If we don't, marriage is often hell. The Christian life is very similar: we come to Jesus and we all have to make exactly the same cold clinical decision of whether we will surrender our lives to Jesus. There comes a moment, just as in the wedding ceremony, when we actually have to verbalize our decision: "Yes I will!" It is a decision - it is not a feeling - when we choose to give our lives to Christ. We have to choose to surrender 100%.

In the same way, if we don't give our wife or our husband 100% of ourselves, marriage just doesn't seem to work. You can't say "I give my life to you, but I'm going to have a few other relationships on the side." I tell you, if you said that, you'd be in big trouble! You can't do that with Jesus either. We need to verbalize to Him: "Father, today I am surrendering everything, and I'm giving my whole life over to Jesus. From this moment, He is my Lord and my master!"

This total surrender of our lives mysteriously fuses us together and makes us "one", both in marriage and in the Christian walk. We become "one in flesh" with our husband or wife, but "one in spirit" with Jesus. This is a mystery. We become "one in spirit" when we make that commitment. This is extraordinary, but what stops it working is when that "little me" refuses to die. That is why Paul in Romans 6 says: "Listen, for this life with Christ to really work in you, you've got to "reckon yourself dead to sin"". Now that word "reckon yourself" is an accountancy term. It is encouraging us to "add up" a few things in our minds and come to a logical conclusion. Once I have had a revelation of the Cross and seen in my spirit that the Cross really does deliver me from the power of sin and also sets me free from my selfish ego, then I can come to this vital conclusion and "reckon myself dead to sin".

Practically how do we journey through this? Listen to what Paul says: "Have you forgotten that all of us who were immersed into union with Jesus, the Anointed One, were immersed into union with his death? Sharing in his death by our baptism means that we were co-buried and entombed with him, so that when the Father's glory raised Christ from the dead, we were also raised with Him. We have been co-resurrected with him so that we could be empowered to walk in the freshness of new life. For since we are permanently grafted into Him to experience a death like His, then we are permanently grafted into Him to experience a resurrection like His and the new life that it imparts. Could it be any clearer that our former identity is now and forever deprived of its power?" (Rom 6:1-3 TPT)

Baptism by full immersion is the best symbolism for being buried with Christ. As we go down into and under the water it is symbolizing our death and burial. Even those who have been baptized as children by believing parents, need to "reaffirm" their baptism vows by being baptized again, because they need to recognize that, now that they have personally come to faith, their old life is being buried. Baptism is also similar to a wedding ceremony.

Let's look at Jesus as He chooses to be baptized: when Jesus goes down into the Jordan, it is as if Father says "Jesus you've got a choice now. Will you take all of humanity with all of its filthy sin, and will you give yourself unconditionally to all of this foul, independent, and rebellious creation? Will you take it, will you love it, and will you cherish it?" As Jesus went down into the waters of the Jordan, He was shouting out: "Yes! Yes! Yes! I will! I am giving myself 100% to humanity." That is why when He came up out of the water, God shouts out with a father's pride: "Now, this is My beloved Son! I'm so thrilled with His choice today!" because He knew His son would not pull back from the very reason He came to earth – to rescue mankind from sin and from Satan. God knew that His Son was a chosen vessel who had made the choice to take all of mankind's sin upon Himself. It was a choice: Jesus had the choice, and He chose to give himself fully into that baptism, symbolizing that there was a wedding and a bonding happening. Jesus was covenanting himself to humanity: he was giving Himself totally to us.

So, when each of us is baptized, we complete the picture. It's as if Father is saying: "After what Jesus has done, will you now take Jesus to love, to honour, and to obey?" As we go into those waters of baptism, we are saying "Yes! Yes! Yes! I'm yours, Jesus!". At that moment we are bonded together with Him, and together we become "one in spirit with Christ". This is the key to life - dying to our self and giving everything to Him.

This first symbolism of baptism is about becoming bonded, or fused together, with Christ. The second symbolism is about the death and burial of our "old man". When Jesus was crucified, my old self or my "old man" was crucified with Him. What I am talking about is all of that old "stuff" that used to grip me and hold me captive to my adamic nature, my hereditary past, and my personal sin and choices: all this is stripped away and cut away from me, and then I give it a good burial in those baptism waters. When I come up out of the water, I don't have to be gripped with that anymore; I don't have to even refer to, acknowledge, or even look at all that "stuff" anymore. Jesus shouted: "It is finished! If anyone is in Christ then they are a new Creation. The old has gone!" It is so important to recognize that in Christ I'm cut off from all the past.

The third part of the symbolism, as we come up out of the water, is that because Jesus rose again, I rose with Him as a "new creation". What is this "new creation?". This is so important, because there are many Christians who believe that our Christian life should just mirror the life of the "man Christ Jesus". That is not what the Bible says: it says that Jesus was "the last Adam" and as the "last Adam", Jesus went into death and He took all of the sin of Adam's race onto Himself. It's extraordinary to even think about how He did this on the Cross.

Now, please don't slam the book shut as I make the next statement: the central core of the Christian faith is not just that Jesus rose from the dead. After all, Lazarus was in the grave longer than Jesus, and after the resurrection many other dead people were actually seen walking around, and some people were even raised from the dead in the Old Testament. No one has built a religion around them, in fact none of them are still with us, because they were all still subject to the law of sin and death.

No, the core of our world-changing message is how Jesus came back from the dead! He came back as "the second man" – a totally brand-new creation, which Paul calls "the man from heaven!" (1 Cor 15:49) He was no longer subject to the "law of sin and death", He was no longer subject to sin, sickness, the curse, poverty, or anything else which was part of the "human condition". It is this "new creation" that is alive in us at the very moment that we come into Christ by faith! This is the image that we are called to bear as Christians. This is who we reflect, not merely the "man Christ Jesus." This is a completely new creation, and this is the One I am bonded with through baptism. This is the One that I am clothed with! I am clothed with His power and His glory, with access to all His life, His weapons, His gifts, and His riches, and His authority. Now how on earth does that become possible simply by faith?

All this is possible because of one spiritual law. It is what we call the law of "generational transfer" or the "law of heredity". As a believer, it is very important to understand that this is an unbreakable spiritual law. This answers the question "How can an event two thousand years ago affect me today? How and why does that work?" Let's look at a man called Melchizedek, whom we see in Heb 7:9-10. In this passage it says: "one might even say that Levi who collects the tithe, paid the tithe through Abraham. For although Levi was yet unborn, the seed from which Levi came was present in Abraham when he paid his tithe to Melchizedek."

What Paul is saying here is that Levi wasn't even born when Abraham paid tithes to Melchizedek, but it still affected his future. He wasn't born yet, but his ancestor Abraham did something which Levi had nothing to do with - yet it totally affected his future! This law is very clear and we can often see it when we are being counselled: whatever my ancestors did and whatever is in my physical or spiritual past and lineage, will affect me today both for good and for bad. If I marry into royalty, this will have a huge impact on my kids. They have no choice about it, but similarly if I had been involved in some form of notoriety, my kids would also have had to bear the consequences of that in the future.

We must try to understand this: that whatever has happened in my family lineage will affect me for good or bad. If I choose to get divorced, it is not just a personal thing. This is going to affect history. It's going to affect my kids, my grandkids, and even my great grandkids. This is going to hugely impact the future. Whatever is in our lineage will affect us both for good or bad. We will inherit either a blessing or a curse. Yes, we can be blessed by past generations, but we can also be cursed.

There is such a thing as a "relentless generational blessing" which will pursue you if you had a generational line that was honouring and obeying God. You can suddenly find yourself as a child being swept off your feet by the blessing of God. I have been unbelievably blessed in my life because of past wonderful saints in my background. Even if I say: "I just don't deserve it!", God's "law of generational transfer" or "heredity" means that I will be blessed because of the godliness of my ancestors. Like Levi, I was "in them as seed" even though I wasn't yet born.

Can you understand what I'm saying? Sadly, the same is true if my forefathers have been involved in witchcraft or freemasonry or there has been a divorce, murder, or something negative has happened in past generations: all this will also affect me. So, we will inherit both blessings and curses from our ancestors, whether or not we are believers. The Bible says however that the moment we come into Christ, all the past generational curses are broken by faith. By faith we can believe that all of our negative hereditary line can be broken when we come to Christ.

In the same way that I was "in the loins of Adam" when he sinned and so inherited a sinful nature, I was also "in Christ" by faith when He died and rose again as the "man from Heaven". When Jesus died on the Cross and paid for sin, I was part of Him. By faith I can be part of Him right now as well. That is how it can affect us in our day. I wasn't there in that chronological time, but I was there in seed form by faith. *All this comes by faith*: just as I was there when He died, and I was there when He paid for my sin, so in the same way, I was there when He was raised.

That's why this is a "faith thing" from first to last - it is not "make believe": by faith it can be activated.

Once you "see" this and you accept all this by faith, you will certainly be transformed! Romans 6:5 says that "by faith we were baptized into Christ." Now that means being baptized into the lineage of Christ. So, when I go into that water, I am not only being baptized to symbolize my death, but I am also being connected to His lineage! I'm being baptized *into* Christ. We are immersed into Him, put into Him and by faith we are then part of everything that He's experienced both in death and resurrection. Can you see and understand this? Grasping this by revelation is life changing!

CHAPTER 16

THE FINAL STRUGGLE OF OUR SELF-LIFE

In Galatians 2:20 Paul was able to shout out with joy: "I have been crucified with Christ, so I no longer live, but Christ lives in me and the life I now live in this body, I am living by faith in the Son of God who loved me and gave himself for me!" This is all by faith and what an incredible thing it is! When I finally saw this second stage of the Cross, I was able to say with Paul that I too have been crucified with Christ. The "little me" that controlled me no longer lives, but instead Christ lives in me! Every day I am living by faith with His resurrection life flowing into and through me; every day I can trust him for His grace, His power and His gifts.

When Jesus was raised, He was raised as "the heavenly man" - not the "earthly man": this is so important for us. The Bible says in Rom 6:5 "certainly also *we are His resurrection!*" It's not just "in the likeness of that resurrection". The actual text says: "certainly also *we are His resurrection!*" There's something of His resurrection life that is imparted into us; it is "in us" and it is "on us" and flows "through us" - it's what we carry! This is the "resurrection life" and power that is in me. This may sound like a stuck recording, but we must believe that because He died, so we died; because He rose in power, so in the same way, we rose with the same spiritual clothing and that is the image that we are bearing and reflecting.

The question we receive all the time in counselling is "How do I know I'm dead?" We need to let God search our hearts, and then we can ask ourselves the questions, "Am I really dead to myself?"

If I am dead to myself then why do I still try and hide what's going on inside me? Why do I still try and justify myself? Why do I still try to make excuses for myself? Why do I just keep on living all the time worried about what's going to happen to "little me?" Why am I still trying to succeed in terms of "little me" trying to prove myself?

I lived for so many years just trying to prove myself and I know many Christian people who are still living as if they are just treading water, trying to keep their heads above water, and trying to prove "I can do this." That is the refrain of our ego-self, our "little me": "I can do it. I can do it!" Sometimes we just need to fail or sink down to a place where we finally connect with the knowledge that we can't do it – but God can do it *through us*.

There is a great English expression that "dead men have no toes." In other words, if somebody is dead to themselves, you can't offend them: you can't tread on their toes and get a reaction. Some Christians are like that: it doesn't matter what you do to them, they just won't get offended. It's because they're dead to themselves. Dead men have no feeling in their toes, but if you find that there's something in your flesh that keeps on reacting, you have to recognize "there's something in me that needs to be put to death. Something needs to be dealt with".

I went through a testing time a few years ago: it was a time of incredible hardship, being falsely accused, being lied about, and being accused of lots of nasty "stuff." Everything in my flesh screamed "it's not true! It's not fair! it's all wrong!" As I was reading the Bible one morning, I read that wonderful scripture in 1 Peter 1:23, that talks about Jesus. This is Peter writing because he had a revelation that helped him understand something about Jesus. He says this, "when Jesus was insulted, he didn't retaliate; when Jesus suffered, He didn't issue any threats. He just entrusted himself to the one who judges justly." It hit me deeply in my spirit, and I realized there was still a large part of "little me" that hadn't died!

THE FINAL STRUGGLE OF OUR SELF-LIFE

I just felt God say "Just keep quiet: don't say a word in reaction! Just honour those people who are maligning you." I also felt a strange thing, that God was saying just to me: "you don't get many opportunities for your self-life to be crucified like this, so don't miss this opportunity!"

You see, I hadn't realized as a church leader, how much of my flesh life had come back, and how much "little me" had grown back again. So, I just had to shut up and tell the church to honour the people who were maligning me. I had to tell others who were campaigning on my behalf to stop it. You know, this experience really did something deep inside me, because I realized that even as leaders, it's still possible to let our flesh-life grow again. The "little me" just wants to live; "little me" just wants to look good; "little me" wants to look holy – I'm sure you know what I'm talking about. We all do it, but we must recognize that we have to die to ourselves. There's a great saying which impacted me: "Some Christians die without ever really living, because after salvation they continue to live without ever really dying".

As we close this chapter, let's ask ourselves: "Have I been crucified by faith? Have I as a Christian, "reckoned myself dead" to sin? Do I know that I'm bonded eternally with Jesus? Do I know that my "old man"- that "little me"- is rendered powerless and has been buried through baptism? And do I really experience the power of the new creation – the power of the "man from heaven" – coursing through my veins? Or am I still tied to that rotting corpse of my past because of my unbelief?

The truth is, so many people won't let this part of them be challenged. The key in so much counselling is the breakthrough which comes from being able to recognise the truth of 2 Corinthians 5:17: "that if anyone is in Christ they are already a new creation." This was written as if it was a town crier shouting out: "Anyone in Christ? You're a new creation! The old is gone! The new has come!"

We are tempted all the time to say: "I can't believe that the old has really all gone." Why not keep declaring over your self-life: "It is written! The Cross has rendered all that "old me" powerless. I am walking away from it." Remember though that the Bible says that "we work out our salvation from the inside out." I remember when I suffered with PTSD in the Army, it took me 18 months before healing was fully manifested in my life, even though I'd had a profound encounter with God which had delivered me from a spirit of fear. Patience, patience, patience! God says that it's through faith and patience that we inherit all His promises.

Some of us are pretty rough on the outsides when we come to Christ. It can take months for the salvation and the new creation to permeate every part of our life, and for our lives to be transformed. In fact, for much of our lives, we are a "work in progress!" We need to commit to "the journey of the Cross": it is a journey of our lives which changes our hearts, our minds, and our emotions. Our behaviour and attitudes slowly change even though we know that the new creation is definitely alive and well within us and it will eventually permeate all of our being; but it's a process, and we have to work with that process using God's stepping stones to freedom.

We have to first recognize that we can't work it out ourselves: we have to activate it by faith. Even if you think you can work it out psychologically, don't even go there: you can't work it out intellectually, or psychologically. We just have to believe that the Cross has done it all. "I am already a new creation. The old is gone!" It's only obtained by faith and too many people refuse to believe that. We must die to that old wound, die to that abuse, die to that rejection, die to that guilt, die to that shame, die to all the stuff that keeps on trying to make us look backwards, lose faith, and walk into our shadows.

We need to recognize that "looking back" is mesmerizing, as our past keeps trying to turn our faces back to make us walk into our shadow. No! We have to keep our eyes fixed on Jesus. This is so crucial: daily we must fix our eyes on Jesus, not allowing those thoughts, or dreams or nightmares to keep on haunting us. At times we may need to speak directly to it! "Get off me! All these rotten stinking thoughts of my "old man" - you don't belong to me, and I don't belong to you! You have no legal right to hold me. All of that past life is on the Cross!"

Then we begin to walk out of it. Oh, what a salvation! What a salvation! What a salvation when all of that past is cut off, and we can walk out as a new creation in Christ. The peace and freedom is unbelievable when you know that all of your past self-life has been cut off on the Cross. Hebrews gives an amazing concept: it says that we have to "struggle" or "wrestle" to enter into His rest! It is a fight, but oh, it's worth it!

CHAPTER 17

THE DAILY WALK OF THE CROSS

"SELF" ON THE CROSS DAILY
Saved from the **power of Self** ruling through my "flesh"

As we come now to the third stage of the Cross, we have journeyed through experiencing the *first stage* which leads us into *a freedom from slavery to Satan* knowing that *Jesus on the Cross* has broken that hold on us, by paying the price for us with His blood. We have then journeyed on through the second stage which brings us to *a freedom from the power of sin,* knowing that our *"old man - that little old me"* has also been crucified with Christ: all of our wounded past can no longer rule and hold us captive.

Now as we enter the most common part of the journey in this *third stage,* we find *freedom from our self-life,* as it is *daily* brought to the Cross. Our self-life, commonly called the *"Flesh"* is different from my "old man", or that "little old me", which are both about my rebellion, and independence and my past. Our *"flesh"* however is all about our *self-effort*, independent of God. Now this self-effort independent of God can easily clothe itself in religion. We can be serving God, but it can be in a "fleshy" way: what does this look like? Well, on the surface we do feel we are serving Him, and we want to live for Him and to do great things for Him. The trouble is that this can often be mixed with self-effort. We can get grand illusions and begin to think that we can do great things "for God" rather than "with God". Perhaps my own experience will demonstrate this.

I remember when I left the Army and went into business. There was still that fleshy part of my self-life that wanted to prove itself. I thought: "I can make millions "for God". I can do great things "for God"; I can do wonderful things for the Kingdom. So, I set up a Christian company, and made the decision that I was going to tithe 10% towards running a Christian school. Now this all sounds very noble, and it may have been the right thing because God had called me to do it. But the *whole motivation was wrong*. My flesh was trying to prove itself and so I was doing everything "my way"! God just had to face me up with the fact that He needed to take over as the Senior Partner.

Within a few months of starting my business, I was in Korea working with a lot of business directors from Yonghi Cho's church. While I was away in Korea, I was sent an injunction by the High Court: I was being sued by my previous company, who were furious that I had branched out on my own to set up my own Christian company. My wife rang up and said "Darling we're going to lose our house and the company - we can lose everything! It's all over!" So I prayed that morning "what on earth do I do, Father? Do I stand firm and fight this or do I just give in and admit just how stupid I've been?"

As I was walking through the teeming thousands of people in Seoul Korea, I just happened to meet a little group of German nuns as I crossed over a road bridge. As I walked past them, they turned to me, and said in their strong German accent: "We have the word of God for you!" They then held out some Bible markers and they said: "one of these is the Word of God for you today." I took the centre one and was really shocked! It said: "I know the trouble you are entering today. Stand firm and persevere! Because I have chosen the time when I will come to your rescue!"

Suddenly I realized that God was in my face, and that God was behind all of this. I was advised by a friend to go up to "prayer mountain" where they regularly had about 10,000 people praying and there I prayed all night in one of their prayer grottos. God spoke to me and told me exactly what would happen, but it still took several years, and during that time God dealt severely with "the flesh" of my self-effort. Yes, we did win the lawsuit, but more importantly, He trained me in trusting him daily, and sometimes I just had to spread out on the table all the invoices to be paid. I would then turn to God and say: "OK, Father, I've got the message. This is not my company, it's yours. Father, these are your bills that you need to pay."

Sometimes, almost the very next day, exactly that amount of money would come in - because now it wasn't my company: it was God's company. God trained me in faith during those years in business. Many of my lessons of faith were really learned during that business time, being under the disciplining hand of Father God. So, in this domain of our fleshy self-effort life, we must understand that we are not working "for God"; then we can begin to work "with Him" and follow him. We learn to be submitted and obedient to Him.

This third stage in the journey of the Cross is what we call the *"pathway of holiness"*. It's the daily dying to my selfish self-centred, self-effort, fleshy nature. Now Paul talks about this in Romans 7: 23-25 in the Passion version: here Paul tells us that

"I discern another power operating in my flesh-life, which is waging a war against the moral principles of my conscience and is bringing me into captivity as a prisoner to the "law" of sin–this unwelcome intruder in my flesh. What an agonizing situation I am in! So who has the power to rescue me - this miserable man - from the unwelcome intruder of sin and death? I give all my thanks to God, for His mighty power has finally provided a way out for me through our Lord Jesus, the Anointed One! So, I realize that if I'm left to my fleshy self-life, my flesh gets aligned with the law of sin, but now my renewed mind is fixed on and submitted to God's righteous principles."

Can we hear this heart cry from Paul: "in my fleshy self-life, I'm a slave to the law of sin"? In that same passage in those nineteen verses of Romans 7, Paul mentions the word "me, my and I" fifty times! My father-in-law used to call it "I" trouble. Paul had "I" trouble, and that's largely what you and I have to deal with. "I" – my flesh life - must be crucified with Christ. How do we do this? We can only do this by denying "ourselves". As Luke 9:23 says: "If anyone wants to come after me, he must deny himself and *take up his cross daily* and follow me." It is the daily taking up of the Cross against my fleshy self-effort life which changes me.

We need to understand this: yes, my "old man" is totally dead. Yes, I am a new creation, but I still have to submit my flesh-life daily to the Holy Spirit's control. In Romans 8:13 it tells us that "if we live according to the flesh on a daily basis, we'll die spiritually, but if by the flesh we put to death the misdeeds of the body we will live!" It is a daily reality in our lives, and we cannot ignore this part of our lives and assume it will all work out in the end. (The Passion Translation -TPT)

Of course, we all have days when we do get up in the flesh! That is why I find it so helpful to start the day kneeling with Him, and to be breaking bread with Him morning by morning. It means that we are getting up in the spirit and saying to God: "I need your Spirit! I can't do this in my flesh!" So daily we "put to death all the misdeeds of the body" – this means those habits, and all the sexual impurity, the lust and pornography, the addictions, the physical desires, and all the things that we struggle with and try and hide and "put under the rug." It's so easy to put on nice religious facades, but we do need to get real and get honest. The Bible says that "if we belong to Christ, we have crucified the flesh with all of its passions and desires. (Gal 5:24)

Now in real life how does this look? It works in this way, as described graphically in 2 Corinthians 4:11. It doesn't sound very nice, but it just happens to be God's perfect way of bringing us to a place where we can make His love go viral! It says this: "we who are alive, in other words, those who are now alive in Christ, are always being given over to death for Jesus sake - so that His life may be revealed in our mortal bodies." Now why is God "handing us over to death" like this? Simply because the more that death works in me, the more life will be released from me. If I'm prepared to die to myself, my life will be far more contagious! Remember that the grain of wheat has to die before life comes from it. In the same way, God allows us to go through attacks which train us and form character within us.

Firstly, He allows us to go through *attacks from people* and through these attacks we learn grace and tolerance; we learn patience and we learn love. All this happens when people attack us: we have to remind ourselves all the time what Paul wrote to the Ephesians – "we don't fight flesh and blood" - "people are never my enemy!" Our battle is with principalities and tormenting spirits. We need to walk through these attacks reacting in the right way.

Secondly, we go through the *attacks of life* and through these we can learn perseverance and we can learn maturity as we go through these trusting the Holy Spirit. Finally, we have the *attacks of the devil.* This is when we learn warfare, and we learn to grow in faith. God is committed to help us with all these different attacks -the attacks of people, the attacks of life, and the attacks of the devil. But in all of these, I must believe that something good is happening deep inside of me. God is helping me to die to my flesh-life and He is helping me to be mature. This helps to keep me open and contagious, and to allow the love of God to pour out of me. The more I die to myself and my rights, the more life pours out of me.

In all of these, we need to "find grace" in those times of attack. This is a strange truth we find in the Bible: it says in Hebrews that we must come to the throne of grace in order to "receive" mercy; but then we need to "find" grace. We don't have to "find" mercy - we just have to "receive it"! We don't have to fight God to persuade Him to release mercy: the mercy is there for us automatically when we simply come to God in repentance. Forgiveness is there immediately, but only for those who simply come in repentance. We must let God love us and be forgiven – but often more importantly, we do also need to forgive ourselves. The Bible strangely says that we actually have to "find grace" – a step up from just "receiving mercy": this means that you and I actually need to focus intentionally on grace and look for grace, and this means that we have to humble ourselves and come to Father God and learn to pray.

It is God whom we need: we quote all the time that God says: "those who ask, *will receive*; those who seek *will find*; to those who knock, it *will be opened.*"(Luk 11:9); but what the Bible actually says in the Greek is "those who ask - and keep on asking - will receive; those who seek - and keep on seeking - will find;" this is an activity of prayer, and it is an activity for us daily. This is an activity of prayer which allows the Spirit of God to grow within us so that our flesh life is contained. So, if you are asking "why do we see so little fruit"? Perhaps it is because there's so little death in the body of Christ. This is what I see most of all in the western world: I see so much of the "bless "me" culture" – the "I'm worth it" culture – and we're not being violent enough with our flesh life. If we compromise with our fleshy self-life, it will take hold of us.

You may remember Saul and the Amalekites? Saul was told to destroy all of the Amalekites, which are a picture of the flesh. Sadly, he compromised and left one King alive. What then killed Saul? He was finally killed by the very thing he left alive: he was killed by an Amalekite! This is a clear warning and example to us and gives us a clear picture that the very things that we leave alive and undealt with inside us in our flesh-life, these are like "time bombs" inside us and they can potentially shipwreck our entire ministry – even our lives! We all have them: for me it was stubborn independence, and the "fear of man".

Yes, I had the correct theological belief that all this had been dealt with at the Cross; but then as a Christian, I was struggling with things like arrogance and pride, the fear of man, stubbornness, and lots of other different things. God actually says that it's our own personal responsibility to deal with these areas of our life; we have to be transparent – not hide – and bring things to the light and become accountable in that area: we ourselves have to sort it out with the help of friends. If it's kept in the dark, we'll find ourselves living with it and it will get stronger and stronger, and so will the shame. The biblical guarantee of 1 John I:7 is that when we are transparent, and we bring things "into the light", the blood of Jesus is well able to cleanse, purify and deliver us, and this will bring us into even closer relational bonds than ever before.

In my former church in Oxford, we encouraged people into same-sex "accountability groups" so that they could talk about their "stuff" – the guys would talk about their sexual problems, problems with internet pornography, problems in their marriages, and sometimes addictions. They really took this seriously and were honest, and the women did the same. Why was this helpful? Because, if we bring it "into the light" we help each other to walk honestly in the light. If we keep things in the dark, we just develop a religious facade. We must be very careful, because I've watched too many people being taken out by areas of their flesh-life which they left hidden and have never resolved.

I used to send people out to the mission field all the time when I first became a pastor. We sent out about 25 full-time missionaries within the first three years, having trained them in how to reach precious Muslim people. One of our most highly trained couples was sent to work amongst Muslims, but sadly during the training, I totally neglected to deal with their inner areas of weakness. I didn't look with the searchlight of heaven at all, so didn't see what they had struggled with in their past. I failed to counsel them through their past inner struggles, but just trained them in all the mission aspects and in Islamics. Within one year their sexual past had taken hold of them and they were broken as a couple. Why? - because there was an area that had never been dealt with in both their pasts. If we step into the enemy's territory and we're not free in the areas of fear, purity and deception, then it's no surprise if we get taken out. Too many people do get taken out in this way. That is the reality of mission life – it is no game.

I sent another two girls to another nation, and within six months both fell sexually. These were great girls. We have to wake up. In spiritual terms, we never fight people, but we are always at war with spiritual powers which take advantage of areas of hidden sin and areas of our flesh-life which are unresolved. We are spiritually at war and if we don't deal with our flesh and live a holy life, walking on the pathway of holiness, we can become casualties. Now we must wake up to this. I've watched leaders being taken out with adultery, and others being taken out with addictions: I'm talking of leaders!

We see too many casualties, and too many wounded warriors, mainly because they never took this daily application of the Cross seriously. They didn't take up their Cross daily; they didn't deny themselves. The activity of this pathway of holiness is to actively cooperate with the Spirit on a daily basis; He then helps us to "take off" all of our self-life, thus destroying the source of our selfishness and the "little me" inside. It's the Colossians 3:9 moment, when we consciously strip off everything negative before we clothe ourselves with Christ. Too many of us don't "strip off" the negative before we put on Christ.

As a pastor counselling fully adult Christians in areas of their woundedness, it sometimes feels to me as if I'm meeting a little boy or a little girl inside these adults: it seems as if this is who is dominating them and controlling them. So much pain is rooted in our self-pity due to our woundedness. Jesus died to set each of us free from the wounded child within us: we don't need to stay in a time warp, nursing past wounds and hurts. By faith, we can firmly place this part of our life on the Cross. Otherwise it will control us, and everyone else around us. It is so crucial that we deal with the wounded little boy and the wounded little girl inside that doesn't want to give up and die.

Now, I do need to share briefly about "holiness" as there are so many misconceptions about this area of our spiritual lives. For starters, it's not "our holiness" – we are not just polishing up our act! This can end up in legalism and this is very common when a revival wanes, and people's passion for the lost grows cold. Instinctively the vacuum is filled with trying to clean up our act and we can become hyper-critical of others who are not meeting our standards. This is often what generates the crazy rules concerning dress, drink and "do's" and "don'ts" – don't do this, and don't do that! We are not defined by what we don't do, but by what we do by faith and trust in Him.

Hebrews 12 tells us that it's His holiness, not ours. As we allow ourselves to go under His hand of discipline, we begin to share in His holiness. We become more and more "set apart for Him". This is the essence of holiness - to be "exclusively set apart for Him". In this way, we begin to live a holy life in Christ. All we are doing is submitting to His hand of discipline, because we know that He loves us. He disciplines us so that we can share in His holiness, righteousness and peace. We choose to set ourselves apart exclusively for Him, emptied of self, and set apart to carry His glory, and carry His love to the world.

Every day we have the choice either to submit to the flesh or to submit to God. We need to learn to take sides with God against our self-life and against our flesh. Now the reality is that "our spirit is willing, but our flesh is weak": I know in my spirit that I want to go all-out for God, but often it doesn't happen. I want to do the right thing, but my flesh is weak - I so want to do it, but don't. Romans 7 talks about this struggle: Paul says that this is because "in my inner being I delight in God's law, but I see another law at work inside me, waging war against the law of my mind and making me a prisoner of the law of sin and death at work within me."

As we submit to God's discipline, we begin to start living more and more in the Spirit, and other negative tormenting spirits are rendered powerless: such as spirits of rejection, anger, lust, fear, jealousy - the list is endless. Christians can become a landing ground for spirits like this, when they go through times of wounding, trauma, failure, and rejection. We may not be "possessed" but we know that in a certain area of our lives, we are not free, and there is something compulsive which we don't like, and are ashamed to admit. We may well be born again, maybe even "spirit-filled", but we can still become the landing ground for these types of spirits which can then control an area of our lives.

I call these spirits the "ites" after all the Jebusites, Hittites, Amalekites etc, which were always such a pain to God's people, but they could never fully get rid of them. The Cross has the power to deliver us totally; but if we are negligent, half-hearted, and lukewarm, we provide an ideal landing ground for these spirits. As Reinhard Bonnke used to say: "Flies only settle on a cold stove!" So get hot and passionately in love with God! Get the fire of God into you and become a passionate Kingdom warrior, and these spirits will not hang around you for long!

We have a daily choice: we need to get up in the Spirit or else we might find that our "flesh" might find opportunity to take over. In Galatians 5 we see the fruit of what happens when we get up in the Spirit - it is wonderful fruit! But if we get up in the "flesh" we also see that there is a very negative list. I'm going to close this chapter with one simple principle; "You will only walk where you are living". That may sound rather obvious, but if you are not living in an area, you will probably seldom walk there. I live in Oxford, I work in Oxford, and I walk in Oxford. If you're living constantly in a fleshy area in your conversation or imagination, either in your TV watching, your reading, gaming, or web surfing – all the things you do in your leisure time - then you will end up "walking" there.

If you're living in the Spirit, you're living with things of revival, and living in spiritual dreams and aspirations; then this is where you're going to find yourself walking. This means that we need to stop living as many Christians live, with one foot in the world, and one foot in Christ. There is a law of sin and death, just as there is a law of gravity. We cannot play with this, otherwise we are very likely to be dragged down and fall. If we choose to get up in the "flesh", that law of sin and death will pull us down like gravity. But if we choose on a daily basis to get on the Cross and believe the covenant, giving ourselves totally to the law of the Spirit of Life in Christ Jesus, then we will be lifted up. We won't be doing the things that we used to do by habit. But remember - it's our choice. Stay in Christ and be lifted up. As we said earlier: get on the plane, stay on the plane, and keep your eyes fixed on Him! Then daily let the Cross do its work. Following these spiritual principles by faith will lead each of us into a life of victory and fulfilment. It all comes from the Cross, and this third stage of our journey is absolutely essential if we want to live a holy life in Christ Jesus.

CHAPTER 18

SHAKING FREE OF THE WORLD-SYSTEM

The critical moment of covenant transfer

"THE WORLD" ON THE CROSS
Cross over point from minus to plus

As we move forward in our journey through the Cross, let's look at the sign posts of where we have been so far:

1. *"Jesus"* on the Cross saves me from the power of Satan
2. *"little old me"* on the Cross saves me from the power of Sin
3. *"my flesh"* on the Cross daily saves me from the power of Self.

We now come to the *fourth stage* of the Cross and this is *"the world"* on the Cross. Now this is the critical moment of what I call the "covenant transfer". This is the cross-over point from "minus to plus". You can see in the diagram above, that the Cross hasn't been

145

fully turned yet: we've got "a handle on the Cross" but it's still not fully turned. This to me, as a pastor, is the most critical moment, because the truth is that many people don't make it across to "the other side". Yes, they understand the whole concept of Jesus on the Cross, but they never make it across to activate God's Kingdom through their lives.

Let me explain: in Galatians 6:14 Paul says, "May I never boast except in the Cross of our Lord Jesus Christ through which *the world has been crucified to me and I to the world.*" This is a double crucifixion. "The world has been crucified to me, but also I have been crucified to the world." This really is where the reality of modern life hits us. This is where many people live their lives: many people walk as Christians, but they are still captives in bondage to this world system. Now I know we might think that the devil is the "prince of this world" because that is how he is described in 1 Corinthians 4, but this can be so misleading. The devil should rather be described as "being in charge of the world system," but on the Cross Jesus clearly won total authority both in heaven and on earth. Jesus legally owns this whole world: He paid for it on the Cross and broke Satan's hold over it. However, we need to see that it is "the world system" that is still demonized. It is a "demonically inspired system" which is mesmerizing millions of people. We're talking here about the clash of two Kingdoms - the clash of two completely different worlds systems. Everything in the Kingdom of God is opposite to the world's system.

We must realize at the outset, that these two different systems are going to oppose each other. If you want to go up in the Kingdom of God, then you have to go down in service and humility. If you want to live in the Kingdom, you have to die; if you're wanting to receive in the Kingdom, you have to give; it's always different and opposite to the world. If you want to go to war in the Kingdom, then be prepared to surrender and sacrifice, because that is such a powerful spiritual weapon. It's always opposite;

sadly we often use human principles in our churches, rather than Kingdom principles. We can end up organizing our churches on worldly man-management lines not on Kingdom lines. It might look fantastic externally - like a "Microsoft style" church - but this doesn't guarantee that it will become a channel of the Kingdom. These are two totally different kingdoms and we must realize that we cannot afford to allow the world-system to influence us. We are Kingdom people and we do things back to front. Some things never make sense to the world-system, but it makes sense to us and to God in His Kingdom.

This is where the clash happens: in our rationalist humanistic society, people in the Christian world are increasingly having the world-system pervade their Christianity, their principles, and their church reality. We have to be very careful that we don't allow ourselves to be dragged down by the world system. In Romans 12, Paul gives us the key: he says "with our eyes open wide to all the mercies of God (this is the first side of the Cross), I am begging you my brothers, as an act of intelligent worship, to give your bodies as a living sacrifice consecrated to Him and acceptable to Him. *Don't let the world around you squeeze you into its own mould but let God remould your minds from within.*" This is the JB Phillips version - what a great translation! We understand that the world-system is not supposed to squeeze the church into its mould. We as the church are supposed to be "invading" the world with our Kingdom values. So often we see that the world-system is imprinting itself and stamping itself on our churches. Our Kingdom values are opposite to worldly values. Kingdom standards, and Kingdom thinking is opposite to the world.

Let's return to our journey through the Cross: the "normal" Christian experience is to have a "salvation" experience, and possibly to experience in a measure the first three stages of the Cross. Maybe we begin to understand that we can be free from the slavery of Satan, sin and self; but then comes trouble and persecution.

We can see all of this in the parable of the sower: remember the "rocky soil", signifying hearts which have been wounded and still have a few bomb craters. These people can embrace the Cross with great joy, experiencing deliverance from Satan, sin and self; but when trouble and persecution come along, they slowly begin to back off into the shadows.

Then of course there will be so many people who are just "cluttered" with all kinds of life's worries and anxieties, the deceitfulness of riches and wealth, and the leisure-pleasure and comfort life-style. We can start living our Christian life as if on a "leisure cruiser" forgetting that we are actually supposed to be on a "battleship". Christians are at war spiritually; sometimes we forget that there's a spiritual war going on around us for the souls of millions of people. It's not a matter of losing our "salvation", but slowly we can begin to drift aimlessly: we can find that our first love, passion and our first fire, grows dim and we also slowly drift into the shadows.

We can often get crushed by the pressures of the world system. I was in business for a number of years after my military career. I used to watch the commuters travelling in their thousands on the trains down to London. I was watching people just being squeezed by life: some looked so anxious of the future: the whole world system creates this anxiety, unease and insecurity. It was as if they were being squeezed and crushed by the world system. It seems to scream at us: "You've got to succeed! You need to be on top. You need more money!"

It screams all the time in the spirit realm: "You know you can't really trust God! You've got to be realistic - you've got to be reasonable! Come on! You need to earn lots of money so that you can be secure." We have to be so careful, because we have these subliminal voices talking to us all the time, even shouting at us from the TV: "You have to look after yourself – you are the number one priority, because "you're worth it!". Yes, we are "worth it" because Jesus died for us, but the trouble is that the "little me" inside wants to be pampered, and that sucks us into the world system, which slowly quenches the real Kingdom life within us.

The divine seed of the Word of God that first touched our heart will no longer fully penetrate our heart, and slowly we get lost in the shadows. Listen, you may not fully understand the first three phases of the Cross, but this fourth stage of the crossover is so important. We have to wake up because the world system is blinding us as a church. I know the Bible says "the God of this world is blinding the mind of unbelievers" (2 Cor 4:4) but I've seen even in my own life, how the world-system can blind us as Christians. We get blinded by what it offers us, and so we fall headlong under its control. You see, there is a spirit behind money: "Mammon" is a spirit and we cannot serve both God and Mammon. It's a spirit that controls us, and I know how hard it is to get free from the control of that spirit.

I remember in our early years of trying to break free of the tight control of this spirit. My wife and I come from two totally different extremes. I was an Army officer with plenty of money, but I felt guilty about having money so I used to just give all my money away. Rachel on the opposite extreme was a squirrel: she was a "missionary kid" who grew up in India and so she fearfully held onto it so tightly and stewarded her money with fear. Two extremes, but the bottom line was about "self": one was fear, and the other was guilt.

So, we asked God to show us how to break free of these two opposite extremes: one of the ways He showed us was that whenever we gave financially, we would both pray and ask God how much we should give. If we each had exactly the same figure, we would give; but if the figure was different, we didn't give. This disciplined my guilt but also set Rachel free of her fear. Slowly we began to open up our hands correctly, led by and disciplined by the Spirit. Rachel is now Mrs. Generous - I've never met a more generous person in my life! She just gives and gives and gives.

She loves to break people's debts! If she finds people in debt, she prays and seeks God to see how she can pay off their debts. She has completely changed.

I remember the day that God told us to give away all of our little "squirrel nest egg" of savings before we travelled to Africa to work as missionaries. This was a little "nest egg" to make us feel secure, but God told us to give it all away, and to trust Him. What a struggle! I remember that we put our baby in a buggy and walked down the street to give that whole cheque to our Pastor - I think we were tearful the whole way! When we arrived and presented this cheque to the pastor, we could hardly believe his response, as he had just been praying for just this sum of money to replace his old car. In our spirits, we danced back all the way home - we felt so free. Three times in our lives, God has told us to give away everything in order to break the power of that spirit of Mammon off our lives. It was always painful, but what a freedom we felt! The fear of money is very deceptive because it creeps up on you again and again, even when you are in ministry: I found that once I left pastoring with a fixed salary, I felt so thrilled to be back living in faith again. Sometimes when you're on salary, you aren't able to live by faith as much as before.

I now love living by faith but it's still a battle. All of us are at different stages, but we must remember that this dependence on money does creep back again. We have to keep making sure we have the right attitude and just keep examining ourselves: "am I still being controlled by that spirit of money or am I free of it?" By faith am I going to be crucified to the world-system so that it doesn't trap me, but also "am I going to ensure that I stand firm knowing the world is crucified to me?" It's such a vital area of life, which is why it must to be a "double crucifixion" - one crucifixion of the world-system is not enough. In the Cross there's enough power for me to die to my worldliness, but there's also enough power in the Cross to stop the world crucifying me.

One part of the Cross is the power for me to stop being worldly, but the other part of the Cross stops the world in all its attempts to dominate and control me. We need to recognize this biblically in Paul's life. It is very interesting looking at his life: in his "walk-about" going through five cities learning the lessons about spiritual warfare, all hell breaks loose in those cities - they end up with riots, but they also have revival. Paul is kicked out and harassed; he has all kinds of opposition to silence him. However, eventually something happens deep inside him, and he comes to realize by faith "I have the authority in the Spirit to stop this! I'm not going to be vomited out anymore. I'm not going to be kicked out of any more cities. I'm going to put my feet down here. The world is not going to push me around!"

Remarkably Paul begins to stop being thrown out of cities and puts his feet down. He's able to take authority in the spirit realm and persuade the local proconsul to agree with him and side with him. Slowly he begins to realize by faith: "I don't have to be messed with. I don't have to be constantly pushed around!" Now this is the journey for each one of us - it's a real journey inside each of us. Yes, there are trials; yes, there will be testing. There will be discipline and there will be persecution; there will also be shaking, as there is a massive world recession at the moment, and everything that can be shaken is beginning to be shaken. But this is also the time to find out if I'm really a "Kingdom person" and if I really am fully committed to trust God? Is He my provider, and do I really believe that He can look after me now?"

In Hebrews 12:28 it says that "we are receiving a Kingdom that cannot be shaken." Is this a reality in my life, and am I receiving this Kingdom life on a daily basis? In my experience, it is the very act of placing our lives on the altar of God, that stops the world "squeezing me into its mould." Our motivation is always that we have been so deeply moved by the "the mercies of God" in our lives. Where there's sacrifice in our lives, there is also fire; and where there's suffering in our lives, then there is glory. This is how we live in the Kingdom and how we carry the fire of God.

If we look at old Apostle John at the end of his life, he says in 1 John 5:4: "everyone born of God overcomes the world. And this is the victory that has overcome the world - even our faith." It's nothing complex, it's just our faith. We are however not talking here about "saving faith", this is "Kingdom faith". These are two different types of faith. When we come to Christ we are "saved by faith" – this is "saving faith." "Kingdom faith" is different: it is tested by God, and it comes by hearing God speak to you about His Kingdom. When we sow His words into our lives, faith comes by taking that word inside us and then that word is tested, and it grows and grows until it eventually gives birth to what God has said.

There are millions of people globally who are living in saving faith, but it is only in the Kingdom that God's love goes viral! This Kingdom of God is only advanced through Kingdom faith, but it has to be developed and tested. Peter says very clearly that God puts us through tests and trials to "see if our faith is genuine." He's not talking here about our "saving faith", rather he's talking about this "Kingdom faith". What Peter is clearly saying is: "I'm looking for people who have this type of Kingdom faith, that is about far more than just being "born again": they will have the anointing and authority to advance the Kingdom, change cities and transform their environment.

Of course, we all know that God so loved the world that He doesn't want anyone to perish; but He doesn't just want people to be saved with their slate wiped clean. It's not just all about us! He wants the Kingdom to invade everything - every part of the world system! 1 John 2: 15-17 tells us not to "love the world" but He's not talking about people here. What he's saying is: "Don't set the affections of your heart on this world-system, or in loving the things of the world. The love of the Father and the love of the world are incompatible; because all that the world can offer us - the gratification of our flesh, the allurement of the things of this world, and the obsession with status and importance - none of these come from the Father but from the world."

So, Apostle John is announcing that there's a clash of Kingdoms here. What Kingdom am I living in? Am I living with that Kingdom faith or am I allowing the spirit of the world to start squeezing me and moulding me. My Bible says, "Seek first the Kingdom of God and then everything else follows." We have to be Kingdom minded: we must look for the Kingdom and seek the Kingdom.

CHAPTER 19

THE CROSS-OVER POINT WHERE MANY TURN BACK

Now I want us to look at this "crossover point". I call it the "crossover point" because this is the pivot in the journey of the Cross. When you look at the illustration in the last Chapter, you can see that in stage four, the sword is at this pivot point. We've learnt about the first side of the Cross, but we are now at the pivot point: we could go either this way or that way. Let's look at another Biblical pivot point which involved a "crossover point". In the Old Testament there are two major themes: there's a "crossing over out of slavery into freedom" and that is out of Egypt. But then there's another crossing: the "crossing over from freedom into inheritance" and that's into the promised land. There are always two crossings - first across the Red Sea and then across the Jordan. We cross *over out from* something but then we cross *over into* something. So, there is a release from the negative, but always this has to be followed by the entry and acceptance of the positive. This is so important: there are two crossings and we must not miss this.

The Bible says that almost every single person that crossed *over out of* Egypt died in the wilderness. They didn't make it over the second crossing into the promised land. Now in the New Testament we also have a spiritual journey – but this time it is through the Cross. It is two stages again: on the first side of the Cross, we cross over out of *slavery, sin and self*. But then we have a choice to then cross over into our inheritance which is into *sonship, service, and sacrifice/suffering*. This is what we cross over into, through the power of all the promises of God. This is in a similar way, the "promised land" into which we cross over by faith - this is our inheritance.

Yes, there are many people who do get stuck in Egypt - stuck in the world system – and they may never come to Kingdom faith. Often this is largely because of their pride and independence, or perhaps because of their past wounds or fears. They may well be fearful, because once we do come out of the evil slavery to the devil, we do get pursued – just as the Israelites were pursued by the Egyptians. The devil hates seeing people leaving his kingdom. These are the people whom we long to reach with the gospel.

Sadly however, too many Christians are just like the people of Israel; they end up dying in a spiritual wilderness between one crossing and the next - this is the vital "crossover point" we are talking about. This is unbelievably sad when you reflect on the extraordinary sacrifice and suffering that Jesus went through to bring us into our inheritance. They are dying as Christians - not losing their salvation - but never fully reaching the destiny of their potential in the Kingdom.

What I'd like you to realize with me (and this is really important) is that the Israelites didn't get killed by the Egyptians who pursued them. They simply died in the wilderness: it wasn't the Egyptians who kept them there in the wilderness; it was they themselves who chose to stay in the wilderness, even though it was just 10 days journey through to the promised land. They wandered around there for 40 years! My Bible says clearly that every Egyptian soldier who tried to pursue them across the Red Sea was killed, so they could not blame the enemy for stopping them moving forward into their inheritance. There was not one single Egyptian who made it across the Red sea. When the Red Sea rolled back into place, every Egyptian who was pursuing them through the sea, was totally destroyed. This is a picture of the demonic realm.

When we pass through the waters of baptism by faith, this separates us from the demonic powers which are pursuing us. Deliverance often happens at baptism.

So, what is it that keeps us in the wilderness? It is often for the same reasons that kept God's people there: it's our grumbling, it's our doubting, and it's our negativity. We wander around and around in the spiritual wilderness, in religious circles, and sadly we can live like this until we die. The Bible says very clearly in 1 Corinthians 10:11, that these things happened to the children of Israel as "examples and warnings for us on whom the end of the ages has come". Everything that was written down about the people of Israel coming out of Egypt and then getting stuck in the wilderness, was written down as a warning for us today.

The sad fact is that some people do come to the Cross, and are saved from slavery to the devil, but then they go around and around in a spiritual wilderness for years. Entire generations can come and go without a revival. How tragic that we can have an entire generation who never make it through to all that God has promised, and they settle to live without revival. I personally feel deeply convicted as I write this. Our generation has not seen a full revival here in UK for over 70 years (Hebrides 1952) as we have been wandering around and around in our religious circles. Previous generations had people who could push through, and grab hold of the inheritance. Come on, we must break this cycle! Why should we die in a wilderness of religious activity without inheriting the full revival of our God? That's what we're born for! This is what Jesus died for - to bring us into the fullness of His power.

It's wonderful to be saved, and wonderful to be out of the devil's control, but let's not get stuck! Jesus didn't just save you and me out of "slavery, sin and self" for us then to get stuck in the wilderness and die in the wilderness. He saved us so that we could move on into His sonship, and then into the fullness of His promises.

So, let's look now at the two sides of the Cross. The first side of the Cross which we have described so far is all about *God's mercy, and it's all focussed on "me"*. I'm forgiven; I'm free from slavery; I'm healed; I'm delivered; I'm free from every area of sin, shame, self, addiction, and compulsive sin. All guilt and condemnation are broken. Now through all His promises, He restores to me intimate access to Him and the rights to everything in the Kingdom. This is where we come to know God as *our Father*. We experience the *Father's love*, and we learn about Jesus as the *Bridegroom*. It is fantastic, and the blood of Jesus really does work on this side of the Cross – *delivered from Satan, sin and self*.

For some people this whole concept of the power of the blood of Jesus remains just a theology, as they feel they never fully understand it. Let me make it more accessible by giving an example: we have a household cleaning product of bleach called "domestos" which claims that it "kills all known germs." Then we have "white spirit" which deals with paint stains. Similarly, there is only one thing that eradicates the "germs" of sin in our lives and deals with the stains of pain – and that is the blood of Jesus. We don't need to understand how it works, but we do need to believe it works, and apply it to our lives. The Cross itself is gruesome, but simply by applying its atomic impact in the spiritual world and putting our trust in that atoning blood that flowed on the Cross, we get cleansed from all known stains of sin.

The Bible says that if we "come into the light, as He is in the light, we have perfect fellowship with each other and the blood of Jesus cleanses us and washes us of all sin." (1 John 1:7) To take another example: the blood of Jesus is like soap. You can have a house full of soap and still be dirty. You can have a theology all about soap and still be dirty. It only works if you strip off and you reveal the dirty parts of your life – "come into the light" – and then you can actually apply the soap to the dirty parts of your body.

In the same way, the blood of Jesus does have an extraordinary cleaning and delivering impact - but only when applied personally to the areas you know are dirty!

We need to confess where we've gone wrong and bring it into the light - then the blood of Jesus will penetrate every area of stain and hurt. It goes right to the very core of our being. That is why "living in the light" with a small group of people is absolutely essential for staying spiritually clean and holy. So, as I said, this is the first side of the Cross, it is fantastic- *but it's not the full plan of God for us.*

Let's now have a look at the second side of the Cross after this "crossover point" has been reached. The other side is no longer just about *God's mercy*; now this second side is all about *God's Grace*. Mercy is about *not getting what we deserve*; Grace is about *getting what we don't deserve*. Imagine going into the bank to see your bank managers, having come to the conclusion that you will never be able to pay off your crippling debt: you would be overwhelmed if you heard them say. "Hey, we really like you, so we've decided to cancel your whole debt and pay it off ourselves! Get out of here and enjoy your life!" Now that is what "God's mercy" feels like and we dance out shouting, "I'm forgiven, I'm forgiven!". Yes, with this act of mercy, your debt is fully paid off, but you still have nothing in your account.

Grace is so, so totally different! It's like going in to see the bank managers and they tell you that they have cleared your debt, but then to your absolute amazement, they say, "We've made a decision: we are inviting you to become a co-owner of this bank. There's your desk, and here are your keys to access the vault. We're trusting you to steward and distribute our wealth with great wisdom and love for the community!" Now that is Grace - more than we could ever think, ask or imagine! God never wanted us to remain as "mercy Christians" - liberated from our debt of sin, but still powerless to help others. His invitation and call is for a generation of "Grace Christians" who know how to access the vastness of our limitless God, to see a viral move of God which brings salvation, deliverance, healing, and restoration across the globe.

This extraordinary gift of Grace operates on the other side of the Cross and it is no longer about us; *it's all about God and His Kingdom*. For Christ to live, "little old me" has to die. We choose to put ourselves on that Cross, and by doing so, we give up all our "rights", and we choose to die to ourselves. Suddenly the face of God changes: on this side of the Cross, God is no longer just Father, nor is Jesus just the Bridegroom. God becomes *our Lord and our King*: He becomes the One who is in charge. We are now "soldiers under command" with no more rights. We fall into line with the countless others who have chosen to be part of the army of the Lord. This is no time to be sentimental: to be a soldier, I must die to my rights and comforts and allow the Commander to position me exactly where He needs me.

We need to recognize that this is a totally different life experience. God is looking for viral channels of His Kingdom, channels of His power, and channels of His glorious love. We are now compelled by His love. It is a different world. So much of the body of Christ lives happily on the first side of the Cross where it's all about us. Oh yes, it's so wonderful experiencing the Father's love, but if we get stuck there, then the Kingdom will never advance across the Globe. We must put ourselves on the Cross, get clothed with the uniform of Christ's anointing, and then become soldiers who obey the Lord and the King. Then, once we have crossed over, we can begin to start actively advancing God's Kingdom.

This book is really a passionate plea for every one of us not to become mesmerized by the world system and end up being robbed of our destiny. Yes, there is forgiveness, peace, and hope on the first side of the Cross - but it's only the start! In Isaiah 9:2

we hear how the "light has dawned for those who are living in the shadows." Jesus has come for all those people who are living in the Christian shadows. He is calling us to risk everything to carry His light into some really dark places where people don't yet know him. The light of Christ shines on each one of us, and it penetrates through into our shady world.

However, once we are changed by the light, we must fix our eyes on that light, and reflect it out into other lives that are gripped by darkness. Resist the temptation to just walk back into the shadows or get mesmerized by the shadows. We must be very ruthless with ourselves so that we don't get stuck in those shadows and get robbed of our destiny. It's our choice: we may never understand it fully, but the Bible says: "only believe!". Put your hand in the hand of the Shepherd and let him activate your faith to reach the unreached.

CHAPTER 20

COVENANT: HIS LAST WILL AND TESTAMENT

Understanding God's new covenant with us will help us to understand the power of the blood of Jesus. It will help us to fully appreciate the dynamics of the law of covenant. Remember, it is a *law* of covenant, not just a *principle*. Now obviously the Bible consists of two covenants - the old and the new. Both of these covenants are sealed by a "circumcision", which means a "cutting" and the shedding of blood. The old covenant was sealed by the circumcision of the foreskin. Yes, it does sound gruesome, and we are tempted to think "why on earth did God choose that particular symbol?" – but God obviously had a reason.

The new covenant is sealed by the circumcision of our hearts. Something profound and almost surgical actually happens in our hearts; it is a mystery, but something tangibly happens to us at that moment when we make that life-changing decision to commit our lives to Jesus and be baptized as a sign and seal of that commitment. You see, this covenant is God's answer to the deep human heart cry which is within every one of us; it is our faith response when we hear the almost unbelievable good news of what Jesus has done for us and what He has promised for us.

This is what happens with Abraham in Genesis 15 when God takes him outside the tent and says, "Come on, just look up at the stars and capture the vastness of my plans for you and the generations which will flow out of your family line." Having been unable to have a child of their own for decades, Abraham's heart cry is "God, thank you for your amazing promise - *but how can I know that it is going to happen?*". This is often our heart cry when presented with the remarkable promises of God. "God, how can I know that I know that you're going to do this in my life?"

God's answer frames the whole of human history. He says to Abraham "I'm going to make an unbreakable blood-covenant with you. It's not going to be a double-sided covenant where you have to do something: this is going to be a one-sided covenant where you don't have to do a thing - except believe it and receive it." God chose to use a "blood-covenant" as his unbreakable guarantee of what He had promised. This is a contract that is sealed by blood, and it specifies that it will cost the life of the covenant-maker if they ever break the covenant. God is laying His very existence on the line, to show how serious He is in what He has promised.

We see the same mechanism taking place in Christian marriage. Marriage is supposed to reflect the mystery of the Christian life in which Christ is bonded to His Church. It's God's mechanism for divine exchange, which we hear in the wedding vows: "All that I am and all that I have is yours." As we both say these vows, we are mysteriously bonded together and become one, as the covenantal exchange takes place. So, in the same way, when we come into covenant with God, we tell Him the same: "all that I am and all that I have is yours." But what we often fail to realize is that God says back to us: "all that I am and all that I have is yours!" We give him our "dirty rags of righteousness" as we give Him everything that that is ours; but we get back so much more! By faith we can enter and participate in the mind-blowing greatness of our God! This mechanism for divine exchange is also the mechanism which fuses two people into one. It's the birthing of a new creation, with two people being bonded together to become one.

Abram and Sarai are the first two human beings to enter into this covenant with God. Abram is bonded with God or Yahweh and becomes Abraham - Abraham takes part of the name of God. Sarai is bonded with Yahweh and becomes Sarah. Their very names reflected the bonding and the new creation. As soon as anyone living on planet earth comes into covenant with the living God, this then provides the legal framework and mechanism within the righteous government of the universe, for heaven to invade earth's space again. Both Abraham and Sarah come into covenant with the living God, which bonds them with God and opens the portal for heaven to touch earth.

Let's look briefly at what happens in Genesis 15. To our modern mindset this is a very strange old-fashioned ritual with heifers, goats, rams, doves and pigeons being torn in two. These are then laid out to form a pathway covered with blood. In a two-sided covenant at that time, this symbolized the blood covered way which both covenant partners would walk through after they have made their promises to each other: in this context they are making promises to each other with the understanding that "if we break these promises, let us be as dead as these animals are."

We see in Genesis 15 however, that it is only a one-sided covenant as Abraham is put to sleep by God and is not able to walk through that pathway – God alone walks through after the sun has set, looking like a blazing fire. God is essentially telling him: "This requires nothing from your side: I myself am going to walk through these broken animals, and I'm the one who is making this covenant. This is my blood-sealed promise, and I guarantee that this will be an unbreakable promise. I will give you this land."

What happens in this story is that darkness then falls and, as God passes through that bloodied pathway, He makes His covenant with unbreakable promises. It is sealed by blood and *all He requires of Abraham is to just believe*: all Abraham has to do is to activate his faith and just believe! We hear of course that he does believe, and the Bible says: "it is counted to him as righteousness," and so he becomes the father of our faith. The act of covenant legally enables the full exchange from one party to the other. I remember my wedding covenantal vows so clearly, but they were said very naively! We stood opposite each other and made those solemn vows to give ourselves to each other, including all we owned. The reality was that, as we woke up the next morning, Rachel's car was now my car, and my debts were now her debts! But I soon discovered that from her side she could now sign my cheque book and she was also able to take everything else of mine!

The point I'm making is that this is a legal exchange, and what happens through covenant is that it opens up a pathway in which God the Father can legally transfer heaven down to earth. Legally, in the righteous government of God, this was impossible as the whole earth including mankind had been sold into slavery to Satan through the Fall and it was illegal for God to interfere with human activity. Once Adam and Eve had sinned, we were cut off from God's rule and Kingdom, and were under the devil's rule and authority. So, God had to somehow find a man or a woman on earth who would not only believe Him but also come into covenant with Him so that He could legally transfer everything that was in the heavenly realms down onto earth through a human being.

That's exactly what he finds in Abram, who then becomes Abraham; and that's what He finds in His own son Jesus because God the father longs to be able to transfer the full Kingdom order, power and authority back onto earth. We need to understand that this is the reason why the devil so hates covenant! He fights every sphere of covenant because covenant is the gateway to heaven and the gateway to Kingdom power. If we understand that through the Covenant promises of God we can legally access all of whom

God is, then we can know by faith that we can possess what God has promised us.

An amazing thing happened in the "upper room" where Jesus met with his disciples and broke bread with them. We know the story so well: Jesus is desperate to find an intimate place where He can meet with his disciples and enact a covenantal transfer. So, He sends his disciples ahead and they book this upper room. When Jesus arrives (we see this in Luke 22), He says this: "Guys I've been absolutely desperate to get to this special moment with you where I can make a clear covenant with you all." The NIV translation of "eagerly desired" doesn't really convey the real sense. I think Jesus is far more passionate about this moment as He'd lived in anticipation of this moment for years.

The disciples have no clue that he is literally making His "last Will and Testament" with them to transfer onto them everything that He had fought for over His short time on earth. He breaks bread with them and then he says: "Listen, tonight I have transferred onto you the whole power and authority of the Kingdom, in exactly the same way that God transferred it onto me. I have given you this Kingdom. Take it! Believe it! Impart it!" Everything that He has accomplished on earth in terms of the advance of the Kingdom, He is giving it all to them. He is foreshadowing the fact that He is just about to seal this last Will and Testament by pouring out His blood on the Cross.

As He goes to the Cross, the covenant is ratified and sealed with His own life blood; the spear is plunged into His side, causing blood and water to flow from His side. He not only pays the full debt and redemption price to buy us back from slavery, but He also transfers the whole of His Kingdom onto us. He gives us free access into His forgiveness, His redemption, His vindication and His reconciliation - all the "mercy" of God flows from the Cross.

However, it was not only all of God's "Mercy", but also all of God's "Grace"! He holds nothing back and holds out to us the offer to join Him in this "crucified life" so that we too can manifest His victory, His holiness, His authority, His power, and the fullness of His inheritance - but also with His stigma of persecution and suffering. The Bible is so clear that anyone who wants to live a Holy life in Christ Jesus, will definitely experience persecution; but right now, let's not focus on this! We should be super excited about the earth-shaking truth that God's Kingdom is now available to each of us, so that you and I can now make God's love go viral – releasing His Kingdom salvation, healing and deliverance to all who are willing to receive it!

CHAPTER 21

OUR FAITH: THE KEY TO ACCESS INTIMACY

What I love about the Bible is that it is sometimes blunt and "in your face" – such as the need in the Old Testament for males to be circumcised to ratify the Covenant with God. However, the Bible also allows a holy "mystery" to surround the sexual intimacy of the marriage relationship. Paul clearly calls it a "mystery" when writing to the church in Ephesus. What I want to share with you now, is one of the most intimate and beautiful parts of the new covenant that was sealed on the Cross, but I do want to keep it "veiled in mystery" to respect the whole Biblical ethos which Paul creates when he addresses this subject.

In Hebrews 10:19-20 the writer explains the intimacy of what really happens on the Cross. This passage says, "Therefore brothers since we have confidence to enter the most holy place by the blood of Jesus by a new and living way open for us through the curtain that is His body." What is being portrayed here, is that we are being enabled to enter into the most intimate relationship with God - through the shedding of the blood of Jesus. It says that a new and living way is being opened to us through the curtain which is His body.

Now we know from the Bible that the curtain in the Temple was torn in two. What this symbolizes is part of the mystery. As the curtain is torn in two, it is almost as if God is saying "listen, I need you to recognize the illustration of this holy moment!" We are now able to enter fully into an intimate relationship with God. Just as a man and a woman seal or "consummate" their marriage vows and are bonded together through making love, we are also fused together with God in this intimate moment.

At University I studied primitive tribal customs in Anthropology as part of my degree. What was fascinating was that in primitive tribal groups, marriage was often strategic, allowing for a weaker tribe to marry into a stronger tribe for greater security and protection. So often the son of one tribe would marry the daughter of another tribe for strategic purposes: when these two people came together in the covenant of marriage, the legally binding covenant was only ratified when the woman's father could prove his daughter was a virgin. *So it was the witness of the blood on the sheets that ratified and sealed the covenant.* They would never accept the legal joining of the two tribes unless there was the witness of the blood, proving that she had been a virgin.

Similarly, there were always conditions which sealed a covenant, and that is the whole point of the natural illustration of circumcision. The condition for entering into a covenant with God in the Old Testament was to be circumcised through the natural ritual of cutting the foreskin of a son. This was painful – it cost them something - and it sealed their right to be in covenant with God. Obviously in the New Testament our covenant with God is sealed by the spiritual circumcision of our hearts, not the cutting of the foreskin.

So what God is saying through this illustration is this: "I'm inviting you to come into the most holy intimate relationship with Me. I'm inviting you to come and be part of me, to be intimate with me, meet with me and know me, to be joined to me and to be fused with me; but don't even think about coming into that intimate union with me unless something has happened in your heart. Your repentance and faith will effectively produce in you a cutting away from all that has ruled your life. This is the circumcision of your heart."

What I want you to catch here is that it is simply "faith" which is the activating key in circumcising your heart. So we need to consider whether or not our own heart has been circumcised by faith? Unless we can 100% put our faith in the power of God, our heart won't be free to come in. We come into an intimate relationship with God *by faith in that shed blood of Jesus.*

Paul writes to the Colossians, "in Jesus you're also circumcised in the putting off of the sensual nature not with a circumcision done by the hands of men but with a circumcision done by Christ. Having been buried with him in baptism and then *raised with him through your faith in the power of God* who raised him for the dead." (Col: 2:12) Let me emphasize this: there is only one thing that activates this miraculous change in our hearts, and that is *the active ingredient of faith*. We are buried with Jesus in baptism, but we are raised with Him through this one thing - *if we have faith in the power of God*. It has to be so simple, that every man, woman, or child has the choice to activate their faith and come into union with Him.

This is the crossover point: the point in which we can come in to take hold of God's full promises, through which we can actually participate in his divine nature. It says this in 2 Peter 1: 4: in this way we can actually participate in the very nature of Jesus and escape from the corrupting influence of the world. It is here that we can download into our lives the very nature of God - His holiness, His character, and His life. This is where we cross over from minus to plus: as we move on this journey from one side of the Cross to the other, we are crossing over from the removal of all the negative, to receiving all of God's positive Grace: from sin to holiness, from sickness to healing, from loneliness to belonging, from isolation to intimacy, from barrenness to fruitfulness, and from poverty to prosperity.

Yes, we can get used to living with very little: we can even walk around in our lives as if it is a wilderness, but still happy that we are being provided for by God; this may seem enough to some, but it is not what Jesus died for. There is an incredible inheritance waiting for us; there's a whole new land, and there's so much more that we could possess if we will only make that choice to move across and to come into Him and into our inheritance: it's our choice to believe, to receive and to enter it.

God is saying: "I can do no more. I've cut this one-sided blood covenant with you. Jesus died for you, and you're now free to respond and come into everything that I have planned for you. You know that I've given you everything, but if you're going to receive it, this is "all or nothing". If you want to be joined to me, it's "all or nothing": either I'm Lord of all or I'm not Lord at all." This is not just a small thing like raising your hand and asking Jesus to forgive you: this is His ultimatum to you, to get out of that driving seat and let Him have total control over your life. We must stop our independence and stop our rebellion, giving ourselves 100% to Him and surrendering our life so that His plans can be poured into and through us for the rest of our life.

The salvation message is meant to be strong: it's an ultimatum. It is: "Repent, believe, and obey" - it's not "fluffy" and I can't make it "fluffy" - it's absolutely clear. We have to face up to our responsibility and realize that God is laying down an ultimatum. If we activate our faith and believe, then we receive; otherwise we will get stuck on the wrong side of the Cross, walking around in circles in our religious wilderness. The ultimatum is really direct: "Come and die, and then you will live!".

Let's read in Deuteronomy what God says to His people, which is exactly what He says to us today: "See I set before you today this choice – life and prosperity, or death and destruction, and this day I am calling heaven and earth as witnesses against you that I have set before you life and death, blessings and curses. Now choose life! Make a decision and choose life so that you and your children may live, and that you may love the Lord your God, listen to His voice and hold fast to Him for the Lord is your life." (Deut 30:15-20)

Jesus said to Jairus as he was pleading for his daughter to live, "Don't be afraid, just believe!". What rings out to us today is the same, "Come on! Just believe!". Now this is the critical fourth stage of the Cross - the world on the Cross. Either we believe Jesus and resist the world's system and renounce it's influence on our lives or we will slowly begin to slide back under its influence into the world. Remember that I said earlier that this is the "pivotal moment"? We know when we reach this place in our lives, that we've embraced the first three stages of being set free from Satan, sin and self, but here in this fourth stage, it could go either way.

If we would only allow this "double crucifixion" to happen within us - crucified to the world and the world crucified to us - then we can begin to start moving over into our inheritance and into sonship, into service, and into sacrifice and suffering. But if we don't, then what happens is that we slowly backslide - and to be honest, too many people backslide. We slide first of all back under the world system, then under the influence of our own flesh, and then under the devil's influence. You see, these are the three domains we wrestle with - the world, the flesh, and the devil. It's not that we are losing our salvation, but it's not where we truly belong. The people of Israel were God's people, but despite this, they lived in captivity in Egypt for a long time: it was not who they were as a people and it was not where they belonged. They were God's people and they belonged in the promised land.

Too many people in the body of Christ live in that captivity today: it's the world of the "dry bones" and people dying in the wilderness. As we close this chapter, let's ask ourselves where each of us is actually living in reality today- not just in theory.

Having shared about the incredibly intimate relationship that God is inviting us into - through the veil, and into His holy presence - is this your personal reality? If we do make a clear, bold decision to cross over, we then need to read the small print on the contract/covenant. You see, in the wilderness of our lives, the only enemy we have is ourselves. It will always be my own negativity, my own complaining and my own grumbling, which will rob me of God's best; just as it was all the negative attitudes of grumbling and complaining which made God's people go around and around in circles and never enter the Promised Land.

I always used to wonder why God told the people of Israel to be silent when they were going around the walls of Jericho. It was probably because their problem was in their hearts, and that's what manifested when they opened their mouths! God knew that the negativity coming out of their mouths had kept them in the wilderness for all those years, so He told them not to say a word as they walked around the walls of Jericho - not one single word! Sometimes we have to tell people just to shut up: "Just stop being negative about yourself and your circumstances. Come on! Begin to praise Him and praise Him again. Focus on what God has done and has promised to do."

Praise is one of the greatest weapons in prayer. "Father, I want to praise you, even though I'm going through tough times. I want to praise you even when it feels like I'm shut out or even when I'm shut in just like a captive in prison. Lord I want to praise you even if I've got no money, because you are my provider. I just want to praise you, because I know you've got a plan and I trust you totally." We need to keep remembering that if we change the way we speak and begin to praise God like that, the walls will come down around us and every limitation and constriction will begin to come under the challenge of God. There will definitely be some real situations that challenge our faith, and that is when we nestle back into God's presence and allow Him to take us through. We learn to "nestle not wrestle".

As I said earlier, we have to read the small print of God's covenant with us, because once we have crossed over, something is going to happen! In the wilderness times, we are our own worst enemy because of our grumbling and negativity. However, once we cross over and come into our inheritance in God, we become an immediate major threat to the devil, and become public enemy number one! It's as if hell itself comes out against us as soon as we step over that spiritual Jordan.

Remember how Jesus at the age of 30, the age of inheritance, comes up and out of the Jordan and steps into His full inheritance to possess all the power and authority in heaven and on earth. All of hell is released against Him to defuse the one active ingredient that would enable Him to take hold of this cosmic access to power and authority: *the one active ingredient was His faith*. So, the devil taunts Him again and again to rob Him of His faith: *"If you are legally the Son of God…is that really true?".* Jesus just stands firm and never wavers with unbelief. He throws back the sword of the Word! - "I know who I am! It is written in the Word, and I believe it! ", and very soon the devil has to back off.

As soon as God's people stepped over that Jordan, from then on they were battling with the enemy in city after city, slowly taking ground and advancing God's Kingdom. They had real enemies now and they had to learn warfare again. Many of us have just had ourselves to deal with, and we can't even cope with that. So, what's going to happen to us when we have a real enemy?

We have to start waking up as soon we make the decision to cross over to the other side of the Cross. Matthew 11 says that the "Kingdom suffers violence" - there will be violent attacks. If we want to enter the Kingdom, we will have to be prepared for spiritual warfare. There's no turning back: it's all or nothing, and we decide that we are literally going all out for God. Breakthrough into God's destiny for my life will cost me everything – but what a joy as I begin to witness His power and glory becoming active through my life!

If I make that decision to cross over, I will step over into the final three stages of the Cross: I will step by faith into sonship in Christ, and then into service in His body, and finally I will be willing to sacrifice and suffer for Him, as together we carry the viral Kingdom to the world. What a thrill to be clothed with His glory and carrying His power; we become carriers of His "heavenly virus" of the Kingdom. No sacrifice: no fire! No suffering: no Glory! This can wait until our next chapter, but let's just spend some time praising God right now no matter what our circumstances are.

"Father we want to thank and praise you that we're at that pivotal moment in our lives. We pray that each of us would get a deep revelation of this wicked world-system that has pervaded our world - even our Christian world. We pray that you would deliver us and bring us to that place of faith where we can have a double crucifixion - to be crucified from the world and the world crucified to us. We pray that you will be our protector so the world-system will no longer have the ability to crucify us.

Father, I pray that you will give us such a revelation of faith that we can step across into all that you have dreamed of and planned for each of us. We so long to step into all the fullness of our inheritance, as we cross over into the Kingdom that you have won for us. We don't want in any way to die in that religious wilderness of going around and around in meaningless circles – deliver us from religion and those religious circles: we want to become Kingdom people who advance the Kingdom in our generation seeing revival sweeping virally through our nation and many others.

My God, we cry to you to do surgery on our hearts! Circumcise our hearts as we step over in faith. Do what only you can do, to bring us into the fullness of that place of intimacy, through the veil and into your holy presence. Help us now as we continue our journey into the fullness of our inheritance. We thank you Father, in Jesus name."

CHAPTER 22

ENTERING THE PROMISED LAND

As we begin to unpack the other side of the Cross, let me just say that the first four stages of the Cross are fantastic news for each of us. This really is the Gospel for every single man, woman and child - our own personal "Good News"! The remainder of this book is about how the Cross not only impacts each of us personally, but also about how each of us can then become carriers of this "heavenly virus" to rescue the rest of the world! It is so important that we recognize the parallel with the Exodus of God's people from Egypt, recognizing the parallel with each stage where they crossed over physically, to our spiritual crossing over through the Cross of Jesus. We really need a fresh revelation to get hold of this in our spirits. So, after we complete these final chapters, we trust that you will feel that you can at last see and understand the full expansive journey of the Cross - with all its multi-facets - and really take hold of it for your life.

On our journey, we have now crossed out of slavery to Satan and his hordes of demons, just as the children of Israel crossed over the Red Sea to escape from their slavery to Pharaoh and the Egyptians. Baptism is the clear parallel to the Red Sea experience. Remember that every single Egyptian pursuing them was killed in the waters of the Red Sea. In the same way we can trust God, that when we are baptized, everything that is pursuing us and hounding us, is somehow spiritually confronted by the Holy Spirit. Each of us must believe this and take hold of this truth by faith. Our salvation and baptism should be a moment of deliverance.

When I'm involved with people who have made this vital decision to obey God and be baptized, we seek to bring them to faith that all the tormenting spirits, memories and woundedness of the past can now be discarded in the waters of baptism - the symbolism of them burying their old lives into that watery grave. Then as they rise up out of the waters, it is into a brand-new life, a new creation in Christ filled with the Holy Spirit! We do however give them the full picture - both the good news and the bad news! The wonderful good news is that we encourage them to believe that they no longer need to fear being pursued by the enemy exploiting all their past - all that demonic oppression and the devil's claims over their lives. Jesus shouted, "It is finished!": this is illustrated by Israel finally breaking free of Egypt's domination and control.

However, remember that there was also a journey through the wilderness to get into their inheritance. We do have to encourage people to be strong and trust the power of the Holy spirit within themselves during this season, because they are now going to be dealing primarily with themselves - their inner nature - with its tendencies to be negative, grumble and complain just like the Israelites! Romans 8 clearly says that if we choose to live by this sensual nature and our primal instincts, this will lead to spiritual death: but if we choose to cut the nerve of our instinctive reactions, by obeying the Holy Spirit and believing in the power of baptism, we are on the way to cross our spiritual Jordan into really living in the fullness of our inheritance!

It is so important that people understand that they now have authority in that realm, but it is by the Holy Spirit and not by their own efforts; our prayer is that people will not go around and around in religious circles, still tied to the world system, and almost yearning to return to it; by faith in the spiritual power of baptism, each person can cross over into the fulness of their inheritance in Christ.

Then we must each realize and help other people to understand, that this is where the real fight begins. This is the fight of faith that Paul talks about in 1 Timothy 6. It is important to remember however, that it's a "good" fight of faith: every little boy knows what a "good" fight is - it's one that we win! If we recognize that we've been called to a "good fight" of faith, then it's one that Jesus has already won: but we still have to engage in it. We don't win if we don't engage; but if we do engage, we will win!

There are so many promises in the Word, and they don't just materialize mysteriously without our engagement. Every single promise is won through faith and patience - promise by promise by promise. As we begin to personally claim the promises, the Word becomes flesh in our lives. I know that there is much of the Word that is already "flesh" in my life – it has become a reality: it's real and it's tangible. But there is so much more! We should never rest on our laurels: we should still be searching the scriptures for more and more promises to make real in our lives so that we can possess them. By faith and patience, we have power over Satan, power over sin, sickness, different tormenting spirits and curses on our life, power over our self and the things we have struggled with.

There is however no short cut to experience all of this. There is a clear biblical process sketched out by Paul in Colossians 3, before we can stand with our heads up, clothed in all these wonderful things that Jesus has won for us on the Cross. First, we do have to come to Father and confess to Him all the "stuff" we have been involved in. The picture that Paul paints is that we all have to strip off our old self with all its shameful practices, and only then can we clothe ourselves with His compassion, kindness, humility, gentleness and patience, having tolerance for other people and forgiving everyone who has ever harmed us.

This enables us to live in love and peace with those around us and retain a truly thankful heart. Jesus went to the Cross first, before he was resurrected as a new creation; we have to follow and be willing first of all to die to our old selfish life, and only then can we go on to receive from Him a complete inner transformation with His resurrected new creation life inside ourselves. It's Calvary first, then Resurrection and finally Pentecost: that is God's order and that is the process we follow: first taking responsibility for our past and coming to Him in confession, dying to our old self, and then burying it in the waters of Baptism; only then can we rise up by faith into Christ and be filled and empowered with His Holy Spirit, ready to step into the other side of the Cross.

One of the things that we find very difficult to bring people to believe, is that they can strip away all the shame of their past and be virginal right now - after all their sexual past; it is a major problem in our modern society. People find it so difficult to understand that aspect of the power of the Cross. We need to come to faith in this personally, so that we can then convince others. It is the gift of faith that God gives us that we can stand before God "virginal" - absolutely pure, pristine, clean, white – as a virgin. Many might say to you that this is just "make believe" but no, it's not! We must personally believe that there is enough power in the blood of Jesus to make people who have totally messed up sexually in every kind of act, to be able to stand before Him totally virginal. If we don't believe this, then how could we ever have a message for this generation, because the vast majority have messed up. Please ask God to help you come to faith in this special area.

I remember when my father in law was in New York teaching some of the interns in a large church: he met this precious, really beautiful, young girl who was an intern: she had been rescued off the streets, having been part of the street gangs in New York. She'd been a prostitute for many years, gripped by prostitution all her life. Then she was saved through the work of one of the street teams from that Church. She was invited to join their internship. God had great plans for her life, which she was struggling to believe. Very soon, she fell in love: however, the guy she fell in love with was "Mr. Squeaky Clean" - fourth generation from a line of Pentecostal pastors - all his lineage were pastors or "holy" people. The contrast with her past was so extreme that she couldn't get her mind around it: how could she – a former prostitute - possibly give herself to such a "holy" guy.

So, my parents-in-law prayed for a key, and God gave them the verse in 2 Corinthians 11:2- "I am jealous for you with a godly jealousy. I promised you to one husband, to Christ, *so that I might present you as a pure virgin.*" They sat with her and counselled her for a while and then showed her the verse that God had spoken to them about her. They told her how she could be virginal - right now by faith in the power of the Cross! She got it! In a flash of revelation, she finally understood that God wanted to present her as a pure virgin to this young man. She was able to finally bring herself to accept his plea to marry him!

On their wedding day, she was able to walk down that aisle in her white dress, absolutely radiant, head up high, virginal, pure, with not the slightest bit of stain. Prostitution was gone! She was absolutely pure, presenting herself to him as a pure virgin. Now that is a Gospel I can shout about! What a gospel! This is good news to this broken generation that carries so much shame. If we don't really "know" this deeply ourselves, then all we are preaching is just ideas and theology. This has to be so tangible to us; this needs to be so real that people who have messed up, can actually grasp this revelation, and experience the cleansing power of the Cross. What an amazing God! For this message, it is so worth surrendering my life to bring healing, and reconciliation to this broken generation!

CHAPTER 23

TRANSFORMING POWER OF SONSHIP AND COVENANT

COVENANTED TO CHRIST
Cross over from **Satan into "Sonship"**

Let's now look at the *fifth stage* of the Cross. When we finally cross over after the first four stages, it is all downhill! Things will speed up now! We are crossing over from Satan's grip and control, into the fullness of being gripped by our new "sonship" as we covenant ourselves to Christ. This is where we must now fully understand what biblical "sonship" really means. There are many words in Hebrew to describe a "son", right from toddler stage to full maturity. The word "son" being used in this context, is the word "huios": this means that we are the "son and heir" of the father. It denotes firstly that we have reached the age of 30; secondly that we have the character and approval of the father; and thirdly that we have the right to inherit as an heir. We have the right to possess and take hold of the full inheritance of the father.

Jesus talks about this custom when he tells the story about the Prodigal son. These two sons have obviously reached the age of at least 30, and they both know it is high time that they should be treated as heirs and inherit from their father. However, with all his exemplary character, the older son has zero faith to receive anything from his father, and so the topic was never brought up, and he receives absolutely nothing. Not so with the younger son! He has bags of faith to go and ask the father for his share of the inheritance, but he has zero character. We all know the story – he totally messes up his life and ends up living impoverished and broken.

Jesus is making the point that neither of these two reactions is right, as many of us are exactly like one of these two brothers – either lacking the faith or the character. We need to have both the faith and the character together, as Jesus then models for us; He shows how a truly honourable son of the Father should live: He comes at exactly the age of 30 to begin this process of stepping into his inheritance. He walks down to the Jordan River to meet his cousin John, understanding every aspect of the law of "sonship". He knows that he is 30 years old, and He knows he has the character of the Father, and he knows that He had the right to inherit the fullness of all that his Father owns.

In those days, when the "son" or "huios" reached the age of 30, the father would arrange a gathering of family and close friends. Although it was a party, it was also the time of legally transitioning the father's inheritance to his son. At an appropriate time in the festivities, the father would stop the party and ask everyone to gather around. He would then point at his son and he would say these words: "this is my beloved son and heir!" – my "huios". At that moment, the father was signifying to all those present that he was legally transferring everything onto his designated son - his full power, wealth, and authority was transferred to that son, and the father would then retire and be looked after by the wider family.

When we understand this culture, we begin to understand what exactly happens in Luke 3 and Luke 4, because here we see Jesus coming down to the Jordan to be baptized having reached the exact age of 30. He stands there in the water, after John hesitates to baptize Him. What must be going through His mind? He knows that His real father is not the carpenter but is the Lord of heaven and earth! He is aware of what He is about to inherit; but He is also aware of what it will cost Him. He's facing the deep inner question of whether he will fully embrace the completeness of the inheritance of His divinity as well as His humanity, by being baptized as a sign of His total commitment to being "married" to humanity, and willing to embrace all their sin. This was the moment three years before the Cross, when He indicated to His Father in heaven that He was willing to go through with it and prepare Himself as the clock ticked down towards that fatal moment when He would sacrifice Himself on the Cross for all the sin of the human race! What a tense moment of choice!

As Jesus makes the right choice and goes under the water, His Heavenly Father calls all of heaven and earth to be witnesses. Then as Jesus comes up out of that water, heaven opens, and Father pours out His Spirit on His Son; the Father shouts down: "I want you all to be witnesses: this is my beloved son and heir! I am so pleased with Him that He's made the right decision!" At that moment, as the Spirit comes upon Jesus, all the power, wealth, and authority of God the Father is invested into His Son on earth. Now for the first time in human history there is a human being standing on Earth, who legally has access to the fullness of the throne of Grace: all of heaven's power and all of its authority can now be accessed by Him.

That's why the alarm bells go off in hell! That's why every demon is mobilized to try and steal from Him the one thing which gives

Him access to the fullness of that inheritance – *this is His victory, as it is ours; it is simply His faith in the legal rights of his Sonship.* Knowing this background, it is no wonder that the devil tries every way to tempt Him during those 40 days in the wilderness. The devil taunts Him, "If you are the Son of God?" Three separate approaches to test his body, mind, soul and spirit. He went into that wilderness full of the Spirit, but having withstood the devil's attacks, He comes out in the power of the Spirit!

You and I are no different when we are baptized into Christ: we step by faith into our legal status of sonship with all its rights of inheritance. As we are filled with the Spirit of God we know that this is just like a marriage ceremony. God says to each of us "All that I am, and all that I have, I give to you." In the same way as Jesus our forerunner, the Holy Spirit leads each of us into a wilderness time as soon as we step over into this sonship by faith. Then all hell breaks loose, and we find that the devil keeps on saying to us: "Who do you think you are? This is just make-believe! There is no way that you can step into that sonship!" You see, all hell will break loose against us, in order to tempt us to doubt that we have the legal right of access into the power and authority of God's Kingdom.

We must understand what is happening here: we are crossing over into the fullness of His inheritance and the fullness of His sonship. Many millions of people have come to a saving faith in Jesus and they have come through to experience salvation: they often do live very good Christian lives, however there are also many who, in spite of knowing Jesus, sadly never activate Kingdom faith and receive their rightful inheritance and sonship: they never fully understand that there is an incredible inheritance waiting for them!

Spurgeon, the famous London "Prince of Preachers" of the 1800's, used to tell a story about an impoverished woman he used to visit who couldn't even read. This woman who came to his church lived in dire poverty and so she was looked after by the Church. When she died, Spurgeon himself went with others to sort out her house.

What shocked him was the discovery of something in her house which he had never noticed before. It was a document which she had framed and hung on the wall. As Spurgeon took it down and studied it, he discovered it was a very ornate "Last Will and Testament". She had been given an extraordinary inheritance, but she couldn't read. She thought it was such a beautiful document, so she just framed it! She had no clue that she could legally inherit a vast fortune! She sadly died in poverty, never entering into the fullness of her rightful inheritance.

That is a picture of so many of us! We frame our baptism certificate and we may even eulogize about the Christian life and the joy of knowing Jesus - but then perhaps we are never able to access all that this means. We need to enter it by faith and actually begin to allow it to manifest in our lives.

In Galatians 4:1 Paul talks of three types of people who may live in a house - the slave, the owner of the house, and then the son and heir of the owner. Listen to what he says: "what I'm saying therefore," says Paul, "is that as long as the heir of the house is just a child (a toddler), *he is no different from a slave, although he owns the whole estate.*" There are many people who are still living like "slaves"- just like I was for 18 months at University; I was still a "slave" – or non-Christian – even though I was in the Christian Union, going to church, singing the songs, but I was still not born-again, even though I knew the Bible better than most, as I had read right through the Bible in seeking to disprove it!

You see, we can be in the house of God but still be enslaved; then we can also be like the estate owner's child or "toddler" (the word here is "nepios") - a little toddler, wonderful, beautiful, born-again, but hasn't got a clue that one day he will own the whole estate! In reality this son seems "no different from a slave"; the fact is that for an onlooker watching the lives of many Christians, they might reasonably conclude that they don't see any difference in lifestyle between the son and heir, and the slave (the Christian and non-Christian). There is no real difference, because neither of them believes they have access to the full wealth and authority of the estate.

"Sons" biblically are both male and female: the "huios" son and heir, is both male and female, because Paul says clearly in Galatians that "in Christ - the son of God - there is neither male or female." We are called to be "mature sons", in order to gain access to the fullness of our inheritance: we will look different and we will live different; we will carry a Presence; there will be something about us and people will think we're different. But what Paul is saying to the Galatians should put the fear of God in us! If we refuse to mature and live by faith and we simply stay as a "child", then we can actually end up living no different from "a slave" or non-Christian. We may be born again, but as long as we stay childish in our faith, we are living with no more faith than a non-Christian – although the inheritance is right there for us, we are unaware of it and unable to access it. Yes, we may well have "saving faith" but we have no "kingdom faith" that can advance the Kingdom and actually take hold of the inheritance.

The moment you and I cross this spiritual Jordan is the moment we say "right! - that's it - I'm all in now! I'm going to stop messing around, going around in religious circles, and I'm going to go all out for God!" The moment we do that, all hell will break loose against us and we will have to fight exactly the same battle of faith in the wilderness that Jesus had to fight. It will seem like every demon in hell is there in our face, trying to make us feel that we are stupid, and we are insignificant. The devil will be mocking us, trying to make us doubt that we have the legal right to be "sons of God" with the right of access to the full inheritance.

Again, I stress that it is all men and all women and all children too, that have the right to inherit. Galatians 3:26 tells us that all of us - that means both men and women - become the "mature sons of God" through one thing - it is entirely *"through faith* in Jesus Christ". "For all of you who were baptized into Christ, have clothed yourselves with Christ." When we are baptized into Him, we are clothed with Him. "Christ" means "the anointed one", so we are clothed with the "anointing": "something" comes on us which makes us look different!

Provided we give Him everything, He then offers us everything, because this is a covenantal exchange. In those days, a biblical covenant was entered into very formally with a ceremony or rite of passage, which gave people the framework for making a covenantal contract which would bind them together as one entity. You can see this with David and Jonathan when they made a covenant together which bound them as one: they would exchange cloaks and often exchange weapons, before they then made their promises of commitment to each other.

As we become willing to give Him our whole life - to give Him everything – He in turn gives us everything! We give God our "cloak" and "weapons" - all our "filthy rags of righteousness", and all our puny excuses and our weapons of self-defence. He then gives us His "mantle of anointing"! We become clothed with Christ, clothed with His authority. Something is actually taking place: the exchange of "weapons" is as if we were saying to God "I'm not going to defend myself anymore or make any more excuses. I'm so sorry, but I was wrong: I'm asking you to forgive me, cleanse me, and clothe me afresh with your Spirit." We take on His weapons instead!

You see this in 2 Corinthians 10: "the weapons that we fight with are not fleshy, human weapons. They are from God and they are mighty for the pulling down of strongholds!" We've got His weapons – so let's stop fighting with our own weapons of self-defence because of our insecurity and our lack of really knowing our true identity in Him. We fight with the spiritual weapons of Christ.

The next part of this covenantal exchange is that they would exchange their names. Do you remember how Abram became Abraham, as the "yah" of Yahweh was mixed into his name, and also Sarai became Sarah? So, in the same way, in this joining of names, we take onto ourselves the name of "Jesus". We often pray the words "in the name of Jesus", and this is not just an empty meaningless ritual: this signifies that we are now standing in the place of Jesus, using His name, with the authority of Christ. Our prayers hold weight. We know by faith that as "Christians", we are "little Christs": this is the remarkable authority that we have. So now we bear His cloak of anointing, His spiritual weapons of warfare, and we bear His powerful name and authority.

All this is sealed by the exchange of rings, and the sign of His "blood". What does this "blood" signify? In those days, as a final sign and seal of the Covenant being made, they would each put a cut on their wrists and then join their wrist together; they would then mingle the blood on their wrists as they came into covenant union together, and finally rub dirt on the wounds so that the wounds would become visible scars - signs that they had made covenant.

As I mentioned earlier, my Anthropological studies at University fascinated me: it intrigued me that smaller or weaker tribal groups would look to make a covenant with a stronger tribal group, so that they would be protected. This often happened through the exchange of sons or daughters for marriage. When a tribal chief lifted his right arm, displaying the scars of several Covenant bonds, this sent a message - "If you attack me, you attack all my Covenant partners! Back off!" When he went to Africa, David Livingston came into covenant with a number of different tribal chiefs and soon became aware of this practice. This may well have accounted for how long he survived, under the protection of local chieftains.

Using this symbolism, let's imagine what the Bible means when it says that "God raises His mighty right hand" when He comes to protect us from the enemy. It is as if Jesus stands up against the devil, raising His right arm showing the scars from the Cross and says "Back off! Don't you even try to mess with these guys! Through the Cross, I'm in covenant with these people!" The devil bows low and backs off, because he knows that he has been totally disarmed by the Cross, when Jesus made a public spectacle of the devil's downfall, as He triumphed over him through the Cross (Col 2:15)

Let's just look back at that exchange of rings, as this might help us to realize the significance of what is happening through our Covenant with God. In our wedding services today, we now mirror the practice of those biblical days as they exchanged rings and exchanged covenantal promises. Our wedding ceremony is a full reflection of these ancient covenant principles, though often the depth of significance is veiled. Our wedding ceremonies have a similar symbolism as the old covenant ceremonies - the covenant wedding robes, the making of wedding vows to each other, then the exchange of names, and finally the exchange of rings, which takes the place of the ancient symbolism of "shedding blood".

Please forgive me if I underline several things here from Chapter 14. As I mentioned, my anthropological interest from University caused me to study this symbolism of the "blood": as tribes joined forces through the covenantal marriage of son and daughter, vows were made to each other and then these covenant vows were literally "sealed with blood". As I shared earlier, the covenant between the tribes was only finally sealed when the man and woman consummated their marriage by making love: the breaking of the hymen would cause the shedding of blood on the sheets, which proved the virginity of the girl. Even today, in some Islamic cultures in Africa, this is still required as proof of virginity. No blood on the sheets, no covenant! I was always fascinated by this. Nothing else mattered: they were not joined until they could prove the girl's virginity. The message for us is loud and clear: *only the shed blood of Jesus guarantees and seals the covenantal contract we have with Almighty God.*

The "New Covenant" is a "blood sealed contract" that we are entering by faith. We're entering something that is quite extraordinary: an unbreakable intimate bond with God as our Father. You will remember that when Jesus died on the Cross, the curtain of the temple was torn in two and the soldier threw a spear into the side of Jesus which caused both water and blood to flow out. All of these pictures indicate the spiritual reality, that the "hymen" of heaven was torn in two as a new and living way was opened up for us in the spirit realm, so that every man, woman and child could enter the most intimate "holy place" of God, to become one with Him through faith. Water and blood also symbolize the birthing of the new creation - mankind clothed with Christ, which we will refer to later.

Let's see how the apostle Peter viewed Jesus's death on the Cross: he saw it as the moment when God came into a new Covenant with mankind. In 2 Peter 1:3 we read: "His divine power has given us everything we need for life and godliness through our knowledge of Him who called us by his own glory and goodness. *Through these He has given us his very great and precious promises, so that through them you may participate in the divine nature,* having escaped the corruption in the world caused by evil desires.".

What an incredible statement! He's given us "everything" - "everything we need for life and godliness" - but it's only through His covenantal vow and promises. This new covenant gives us the legal right and access to actually "participate in the very nature of God"! Through those promises we can access "everything" - intimacy, faith, love, power, freedom, deliverance, healing, provision - "everything"! However, there is one condition: we see it in Colossians 2:11: it is as if God says: "don't even think of coming into intimate union with me, unless you have allowed the circumcision of your heart which happens purely "by faith" in the power of God. Remember that it is essentially "faith" that opens the heart of God to us: that's what really pleases Him, and this is such a doorway into an intimate union with Him.

Do we realize the extraordinary power that we are stepping into when we come by faith into this intimate union with Christ? Let me repeat the statement I made earlier: the Christian message is not just about "Jesus rising from the dead" - that is not the essence of our Christian message, because as I said earlier, other people were raised from the dead both in the Old and New Testament. The difference is that all these other people came back to life but were all still subject to sin, sickness, death and the curse over mankind. Every one of them eventually died and have long since been forgotten; but Jesus was totally different and is still alive!

We need a revelation of the nature and power of our resurrected Lord Jesus. Hebrews 5:7 says that "during the days of Jesus's life on earth, He offered up prayers and petitions with loud cries and tears to the one who could *save Him from death*. And he was heard because of his reverent submission." He was not crying out for God to *save him from death*: that word "from death" means *"up, out from within death."* So Jesus himself was interceding before God His Father, and actually obtained His resurrection to come "up, out from within death", after He had died on the Cross. He wasn't asking God to deliver him from death, because that was His mission; He was pleading with God that once He had died and paid for the sins of all humanity, that He would then be rescued "up, out from within death." It says that Jesus was "heard because of his reverence and submission."

Jesus was raised up out from the clutches of death, as *"the second man from heaven"*, not made of the dust of the earth. 1 Corinthians 15 :47- 49 says that He was "a second man from heaven- a new creation." That is who Jesus is now, and that is who we are! He has legal power over everything; He has all power in heaven and on earth; He is not subject to sin; He is not subject to death; He is not subject to sickness. He is a completely different type of human being – the second man from Heaven. This is how the man Christ Jesus has been raised back to life, and we are now called to reflect this resurrected Christ: this is the man Christ Jesus that we are part of; this is who we are! We are not called to worship a man who just came back to life. We worship who He is now, as He has come back "up out from death", as a brand-new creation, a second man from heaven. This is our identity in Him!

All this is such a mystery: I find it such a mystery that God Himself birthed the "new second man" just as He had birthed the woman Eve out of the side of Adam the first man. In the same way, God birthed "the second man- the new creation" out of the side of his son: as the spear was thrust into His side, out flowed "blood and water" – symbolizing birth from a womb. The new creation was birthed as the "bride of Christ". This new creation that we are a part of, was birthed out of the side of Jesus in the same way that Adam's bride Eve was birthed out of the side of Adam. This is who we belong to as the Church of Jesus Christ. This is the power of the "good news" we are sharing with people. We are no longer subject to the curse of sin, sickness, and death and all the other limitations of the "first Adam". We may not know it right now, because we are looking at it through our normal human lens. Somehow, we have to embrace all this by faith.

John 19:34 talks about how one of the soldiers pierces Jesus's side with a spear bringing a sudden flow of blood and water. God obviously makes John look at this and realize that this is significant. What is significant about blood and water: it is the birthing of a new creation as the waters are breaking. A new creation is being born: this is who we are part of, a new creation, the resurrected Christ that we clothe ourselves with. As the Bible says, "if anyone is in Christ they are that new creation. The old has gone and the new has come." (2 Cor 5:17) That is how clear and how clinical this statement is: it's not saying "maybe" or "some". It is declaring that *"if anybody is in Christ by faith*, the old has gone, and the new has come." We are right now "a new creation" – not waiting till we get to heaven. There is something different about us! We are carrying the "heavenly virus" – the contagious life of the "heavenly man"! What a salvation!

Wow! We should be jumping up and down! What a salvation - it is almost unbelievable! This is what we become, when we embrace the Covenant and we come by faith into our Sonship. This is the transformational power of the good news that we can share with whoever is willing to listen. This new Creation is what Jesus transferred on to us in Luke 10. He says, "I'm transferring it all onto you, giving you all my power and my authority: nothing by any means will harm you!" We step by faith into that new Creation: we step into that authority! Wow! what a sonship: we must get hold of this by faith and by revelation: it is so important that we step into this Covenant and this sonship.

CHAPTER 24

LEARNING VIRAL LIFESTYLE BY SERVING IN HIS BODY

COVENANTED TO HIS BODY
Cross over from **Self into "Service"**

The *sixth stage* of the Cross comes after we have crossed over into our sonship in Christ and been bonded to Him through our covenant with Christ: now we are ready to cross over into the next stage: out from our independence and self-centred lives, into serving others: *we covenant ourselves into His Body, the Church.* This is the sixth stage where we are crossing over *"from self into service"* - but this is "spirit-led service". We read in Matthew 20:28 that the "son of man did not come to be served but to serve and to give His life as a ransom for many". Just in that one verse we see the final two stages of the Cross: the son of man choosing "service" and then "sacrifice". This is what we are crossing over into: *"service within His Body"*, and then *"sacrifice to reach the rest of humanity"*. We recognize here that we have crossed over into His sonship as the "son of man", and so we come to serve and not to be served; but we also come to give our lives, suffering with Him and sharing in his sufferings – more of that later. Here we see that crossing over into sonship leads us very quickly into service within His Body, the Church.

So, what is this sixth stage all about? What is God's perspective of this stage of being joined to His Body? What is its purpose in and through our lives, when we make a commitment to a local group of believers? It is essentially God's way of disciplining our "self -life". When I cross over into His Body, this means that I can no longer live by myself or for myself. In the same way that I cross over into marriage from my self-centredness and independence, so now when I join a community of believers, I can no longer live for myself. I am effectively blowing out my candle! A new creation has been formed and I am now part of His Body.

Just as in marriage, when we make a choice to live for each other and "out-serve" each other, now in the same way we are crossing over into His Body of the local Church: we are making a similar covenant or commitment with a local body of believers. Just as every bride and bridegroom are imperfect, so every single church is imperfect; now we choose to commit ourselves to a group of imperfect believers. This is where we grow in Christ through our interaction with others. For those who want to live in independence, please hear this: "you will never grow until you're planted." When we plant our lives amongst other believers, we are constantly being shaped by them. We are "discipled" – or disciplined - by the Father through that group of believers. I preach so much about this when I am preaching from Ephesians: Christian faith and victory in Christ work best from within the safety of the Body. We're not called to live an independent Christian life:

I've met too many people who think "I can be holy by myself; I can do it by myself; I don't need the body." This is such a deception! We all need the body because it's in the body, that my self-life is disciplined.

We slowly begin to discover that wonderful dimension of "serving, serving, and more serving." That's what ministry is: it's just "serving". We see in Ephesian 4:16 that Paul says that "from Him - that's from Jesus - the whole body is joined and held together by every supporting ligament, and it grows and builds itself up in love as each part does its work." We grow into unity, then we grow towards intimacy; and slowly we grow into maturity, and into the fullness of the Spirit.

It's "unity" first - that bonding with other people, often totally different to ourselves - and gradually this produces relationships that are transparent and intimate. Through the ebb and flow of all these relationships, we come into that maturity of character, as well as into the fullness of the Spirit. We begin to start "building each other up in love" by using that wonderful secret fuel of "encouragement". This has sadly been lost in many parts of the body of Christ where religion reigns, and where people keep their distance from each other. Paul emphasizes that the body works best as we learn to not think about ourselves all the time, but instead to daily notice and encourage other people, and to build others up through words of life; we make people feel special through those words of encouragement - this is not just shallow words, pampering them with platitudes; this encouragement is telling them from the Word of God, how much God is committed to them, and what His plans and purposes are in their lives.

As I said, the truth is that we never grow until we're planted alongside other people. It doesn't happen by yourself, because God waits until we get planted within the soil of a good local body of believers, and then we are enabled to grow. I remember how

God challenged me personally, as my soul was so wounded and damaged. When I first came to Christ, I found it really difficult to even come inside a church building, as I was terrified of relationships. I used to hang around the outside of the church building because I was too frightened to come into the church, in case somebody would just put their arms around me and give me a great big charismatic hug! Even though I was terrified, I eventually slipped into the back seats of the church because I was so in love with Jesus. I would just close my eyes and fling my hands up in the air in worship. I would just worship and worship, because I just loved Him.

I would have loved to have just kept it simple – just me and Jesus; but somehow in my spirit, I knew I needed Jesus – and His body. The Church leaders noticed me worshipping and after a few weeks they spoke to me after the service and said, "wow, you love to worship! We would love to have you come down to the front and lead worship in the church." I didn't play any instrument at all, but they'd heard God and they brought me out of the back row and led me down to the front to become a worship leader. I was terrified! But it was all a part of my journey of healing and restoration, encouraging me to believe that God could use me. It is a journey and we all need each other. Obviously, having pastored and ministered within His Body for over 35 years, the impact of the Body worked wonders in my life! Sadly, like me in those early years, there are many people who still find it so difficult to just be joined to others because of their wounded soul.

So, we need to be part of the Body of Christ and allow His Body to work with us. Why is it so important? Because we each have a daily choice to either live in "selfishness" or to live in "service". We choose to live either in the flesh or live in the Spirit: it is a daily walk. This is where we experience the disciplining hand of God. Please hear me here though: God is not a "meany"! He's not mad at us, and He's not standing like a strict Victorian father, ready to catch us and whip us! He's a good Father! Every day He is there to affirm and encourage us, and help us to grow up with security, self-worth and a sense of significance. Yes, as with little children, there are always going to be moments when He stops us, and His hand is always there to gives us boundaries, because He knows what could hurt us.

As we humble ourselves under the mighty hand of God, and accept His boundaries, this is how we grow in "holiness." "Holiness" is not being "squeaky clean"; it is being exclusively set apart and focussed on Him, as a child would focus on a parent because we know that good things come from Daddy's hand. As a dog lover, I love the fact that one of the Greek words for "worship" is "proskuneo" which literally means to "come towards someone to kiss, like a dog would come and lick the Master's hand": it indicates a total focus on our Father, breaking away from all distractions in order to be exclusively set apart for whatever He wants – this is "holiness", and this is how we grow in love and compassion, and grow in His righteousness and peace.

This is where our pride, our arrogance, our independence and all the rough areas of our life are dealt with. Yes, there are times when He levels mountains like this, but He's also very aware that many of us have far deeper valleys that need to be lifted up: valleys of low self-esteem, self-hatred, insecurity, fears and anxieties. Some of our crooked ways might need to be straightened out and our abrasive manners might need to be smoothed over, but there is a wonderful sense of being dealt with graciously by God, so that He can come in His glory and find a landing ground in our lives. We see all this in Isaiah 40.

The book of Ephesians speaks so much about how God uses the church for His Kingdom purpose. In Ephesians 4:12 Paul shares how God gives various ministries to the church (apostle, prophet, pastor, teacher and evangelist) "to *equip* His people for works of service, so the body of Christ can be *built up*": what he is envisioning is that each person within the church can be repaired in their wounded soul; the word Paul uses which is translated "equip" actually means "to repair the nets", because so many of our nets are broken and our lives are often full of holes. We often need to be repaired in our lives so that we can be thrown back out to fish other people into the Kingdom.

The other word Paul uses is in Ephesians 4 which is translated "built up" means to "rebuild the house" so that someone can come and dwell: God's desire is for each of us to be rebuilt so that He can come and dwell in us, so that all of our broken relationships can be reconciled and repaired and we can start to find our place within the body. Father's dream is not just to break us out of slavery to "Satan" and then break the power of "sin, sickness and self" in our lives. Father's dream is that each of us will come back into intimacy with Him, so that we can "walk in the garden" with Him and can then reflect His glory out to the world.

These ministries help to "rebuild" our relational networks so that we can be bonded with Jesus and His Body, so that we can then have an impact within our community. This is a long process so the atmosphere of welcome, love, and acceptance are vital in every church, so that no one ever feels they must put on a religious façade to be welcomed into church. God just loves people – that's the deal – no small print: whatever our past, whether with a criminal record or squeaky clean, lower or upper class, rich or poor, whatever our spirituality, physical appearance and agility, whatever our sexuality or mental health, Jesus laid His life down for every single person. However, the face of the church changes as we journey on with Jesus.

First, the church serves as a *hospital*, as many people come in broken and damaged, wounded in their souls, needing to be healed. This is where people are healed and delivered and rebuilt, to be free in every area of their lives. Then secondly it becomes a *family*: as people's relationships are reformed and rebuilt, they bond with others in the church and very soon feel they are part of a growing family. Thirdly the church becomes a *school*: they begin to receive basic discipleship and begin to grow spiritually, as they put God's Word into practice. The Discovery Bible Studies are a wonderful way of introducing them to an "obedience-based culture" of discipleship, rather than filling their heads in a "knowledge-based culture", which is often the downfall in our western mindset. Fourthly, the church becomes *a training camp*, where we begin to get equipped, learning to flow in the gifts of the Spirit, armed with the weapons of faith and authority and brought into our full "sonship" in Christ. Finally, the church becomes *an army*, ready and equipped to rescue other people and bring them into the wonderful freedom of Christ's family. We see people in all these stages in the church. This is the progression within church life: *from "hospital" to "family" to "school" to "training camp" and finally into the "army" of the Lord.*

Right from the beginning of the Bible in Genesis 2, God says "I'm going to create mankind to be a reflector of the Godhead. I want to create mankind to be in my image and reflect my glory – men, women and children who will reflect the very glory of God Himself." This is our calling and purpose: called together to reflect His glory. It's so important to understand that this is what God is looking for in our lives: we are called into "koinonia" – to be "one in life, purpose, and spirit" with each other and with God. Some translate this as "fellowship", but it is far more than this. Then in the New Testament, in 2 Corinthians 3:18, we hear this same picture again: "we all, with unveiled faces, are reflecting the glory of the Lord". We have to take down our facades and remove all of the masks and veils we hide behind. We must stop pretending and hiding behind the mask of being "religious". We are simply called to be people with unveiled faces – as we say, "what you see is what you get".

All together, we can reflect the Lord's glory and at the same time as we gaze on Him, we are "being transformed into His likeness with ever increasing glory which comes from the Lord who is the Spirit."

This should be our experience when we're "in the Body". We live with a transparency, which apostle John calls "living in the light". (1 John 1:5-7). He explains that God is light and if we want to live in Him, we must live "in the light" ourselves – transparent with no dark areas hidden. When we choose to be transparent like this, John says that we will know this "koinonia"- "perfect fellowship" - a union of life, spirit and purpose with other believers, in which we will experience the power of the blood of Jesus purifying us from all sin. This is the place of restored intimacy with Father and with other believers, but also of restored fruitfulness.

In Ephesians 2:14-16 Paul says that "Jesus himself is our "Peace": by dying as our sacrifice, He has broken down every wall of prejudice between us and God, and between us and other people. He unites people who hate each other, by destroying the "dividing wall of hostility" through the Cross. The purpose of His sacrifice was to "make peace" by creating in Himself this "one new man" – this "new creation" which reconciles broken, divided and hostile people together in Him: this is the passion of God's heart. The Cross is the place of complete fusion and reconciliation.

Biblical "peace" is far more than our human ideas of peace: for instance, often when we make peace in our marriages, we just decide to stop fighting. The word Paul uses for "peace" carries two pictures: one is of a broken bone being restored and healed so that the join is stronger than it was before - the bone comes to "peace". The other is of two people with weapons fighting, who not only decide to stop fighting, but actually lay down their weapons and make themselves vulnerable: they then embrace each other and restore their covenantal commitment to each other and become one again.

In this way, Jesus is our "peace": He's the one who heals our brokenness, and fuses us together with Himself, stronger than ever before with a renewed covenant. He also heals and restores our relationships, so that we aren't isolated and alone, fearful and anxious behind our personal walls of defence and self-protection. I like to think of this in terms of potatoes with their hard, dry skins: they may all be thrown together in a bag, but they stay totally separate from each other.

A church which has an atmosphere like a bag of dry old potatoes, is never going to be attractive to the world. Imagine though, when we choose to remove all those skins and facades; when we take off our outer skins out of pretences and religiosity, and we allow our lives to become "mashed together" – imagine that aroma of hot mashed potatoes, anointed (in butter!) and sprinkled with the bonds of covenant (salt!) – now that will draw a crowd! This is the sense of Ephesians 2:22 where "we are compacted together into being a place where God himself can come and dwell." Unity like that is irresistible to God and to people – it has the aroma of Christ!

It is extraordinary when the Body comes together in unity like this. This is what God is looking for; if we want to draw down heaven into our meetings, let's be fused together in unity through being real, vulnerable, open and broken. Can you remember when you first experienced God's tangible presence flood into a meeting? When this happens, it is etched in your memory: after I came to the Lord in Cambridge University, I returned to my military unit in Germany. I took some leave and travelled down to the YWAM base in Augsburg at Schloss Hurlach in South Germany, where I was with a group of young people seeking God.

All of us were desperate: we were all Spirit-filled but we were desperately hungry for God. Some of the young people just didn't feel they were even saved. There were about 50 of us crying out to God – simply, just talking to Jesus; as we did that, we all began to get real with each other one by one. Each of us stood up in turn and began to share intimately what was happening in our lives – it was almost like a group confession. I remember one girl stood up and shared that she felt so hardened in her heart, and she hadn't been able to connect with God emotionally in prayer; she said that she hadn't wept for souls for months and had somehow lost her former passion to lead people to Jesus: "I just feel so hard! What is wrong with me?" Another person stood up and talked about the state of his heart, and one by one as we began to be honest, all our facades came down.

I have no idea what happened next, but it was as if God thought "I like this! I'm coming to join the party!" Suddenly the Spirit of God fell on that little room. I've only been in a few meetings like this in my life – maybe only about three. Literally the heavy presence of God fell on that place: the Bible calls it "the khabod" - the heavy presence of God. Every one of us was physically thrown out our seats and pressed down onto the floor. We wept and wept because God had shown up: He was in the room! I wept and wept as I laid pressed down on the floor, as it was the only time of my life that I had heard God audibly speaking to me. It changed my life forever, because once you've been in the presence of God like this and you've heard His voice, you can't play religious games any more: you just want more of God; you want the reality of who He is, and not some shadow of religion. You don't want anything else and, in a good sense, you become addicted to pursuing God and to making room for the presence of God. This is what motivated David to bring back the presence of God to Israel: he would not be stopped. Even though he went about it the wrong way at first, he knew that he had to do whatever it took to bring back the presence of God. This happens when people get honest, transparent and real: it happens within the Body when facades come down.

That's exactly what happened with Count von Zinzendorf in Moravia, when he allowed his estate to be a place of refuge for

Christian refugees from across Europe. All these refugees were from such different ethnic and religious cultures that they ended up constantly arguing and fighting each other, and it became such a nightmare for the Count. Over a period of about four months he brokered a "brotherly covenant" between them all and they began praying regularly together. There was unity, but no real heart bonding of faith and love in the spirit. Eventually, out of desperation, he summoned them all together one evening and told them that this was to be an all-night prayer meeting, as well as an evening of forgiveness and reconciliation when they would break bread with each other as a sign of renewed covenant. God had marked the day: it was on a Wednesday on 13th August 1727 at around midnight, and as they took communion together, having prayed and reconciled, the fire of God fell. (Can you see that this is a similar script to what happened when the disciples met in that upper room to seek God and get reconciled – the fire of God fell!)

This Moravian outpouring sparked a prayer watch that lasted daily for 100 years. 12 years after this outpouring in Herrnhut Moravia, Wesley was deeply influenced by one of their young evangelists called Peter Bohler. On January 1st 1739, as they met with Peter Bohler and other hungry God-seekers in a "love feast" of communion, the fire of God fell again and Wesley was powerfully filled with the Holy Spirit. The rest is history as the Methodist revival exploded out across the whole world.

Reflecting on these examples, we can see that God's Spirit seems to be attracted when people become broken, humble and transparent, and this starts "in the Body" as hungry believers gather together to seek God. We are talking here about real "fellowship" when all masks are removed, and people become honest with each other. We know that God opposes anything that is proud or has an empire spirit, but this is the opposite - the humble place which attracts God's Grace; it is in this atmosphere of openness and brokenness that God can re-infect us with what I now call His "heavenly virus" - the contagious presence of the glory of God resting on our lives. The glory of God is simply the "outshining" or dazzling reflection of the perfect relationship of the Godhead. When we come into that perfect relationship of unity and oneness, something happens, which ushers in the redemptive presence of God into the community.

We see this process happening with the early disciples who seemed to be fighting each other and competing all the time. After Jesus was crucified, God had to treat them just like children: "you go to your room, and you're not coming out till you've sorted out all your squabbles!" Graciously, the Bible doesn't tell us exactly what happened over that period, as 120 of these early disciples cowered in that place in fear of persecution; but we can imagine that the death of their Lord and Master brought a reality check in their relationships, and that these days were filled with confession, forgiveness and reconciliation. Even so, it still took them ten days before there was an atmosphere of humility, openness and brokenness, which God couldn't resist. He burst in amongst them with wind and fire, and the "heavenly virus" was injected with such contagious power that it swept through Jerusalem and out across the known world at that time.

It seems that there are times in Church history when God throws a small group of believers into an "upper room", to sort out their petty fighting and denominational religious squabbles, and then He comes again in power. Church history has so many examples of this down the ages. There are periods of Church history when it seems that "Ichabod" - "the glory has departed"- is written over the church. Listen to some of Jesus's final words before he went to the Cross: in that intimate time of breaking bread with his closest disciples, in Luke 22:15, He says "I've been desperate to have this covenant meal with you before I suffer." He wanted this meal to be a covenantal meal in which He could transfer onto them everything that was on Him. In verse 29, He says "I've now transferred onto you the Kingdom!"

The "Kingdom" is the word Jesus uses to encompass all the contagious fullness of God's love, power and authority. We actually hear Jesus telling His father in John 17: "I've done it! I've finally transferred onto my disciples the same viral Kingdom glory and power that you gave to me. This will bond them so close together, because they will all be within me, in the same measure that I am now living within them by my spirit." This is the trigger for the remarkable atomic explosion that happened in the spirit realm when Jesus died on the Cross and was then raised triumphant over the devil and all his works.

Anybody who comes into a direct encounter with the risen Christ Jesus becomes contagious. Once we've met Him like this, we are fused together with Him. This bonding with Christ facilitates the transfer of all of His character and nature into us. No bond, no transfer. When we are fused together with Him and His Body, then we become infected with all of His core values and passions, and we fully embrace His heart of "service" within the Body.

It is essential that the work of the Cross is fully worked in each of us and that we become contagious. As I travel around churches in the Western world, it's always a real thrill to find churches and Christians who are spiritually contagious. By contrast, when I worked for five years with the Chinese pastor Brother Yun, who is called "the heavenly man", I soon became aware that his Chinese form of Christian faith is contagious because their entry point into the Kingdom is very different: their entry point is when they each make a life choice to step into "service and sacrifice", where they are willing to die for their faith. For us in the West this seldom enters our minds, but "101 Christian discipleship" for these Chinese is not entered until they're willing to lay their life down. Through "service and sacrifice" they become viral: they become contagious everywhere they go; everywhere people begin to catch it, and they begin to find the glory of God operating in and through their lives.

Let's briefly face this "million dollar" question: "how do we become contagious and how is the Kingdom transferred virally?" I'm sure you will recall that Jesus asked Peter a simple but heart-searching question about who they each perceived Him to be. Like a flash, Peter showed that he'd had a revelation, and he shouted out "You are the Christ, the son of the living God!". Revelation is the key: it's such a simple but essential key, because the Kingdom has to be "seen" in the spirit realm, and this germinates "faith". Jesus realized that Peter had this revelation but that the others didn't, and that's why He said, "on this rock (of revelation) I can start to build my church". Each of us must accept that our human "knowledge" is not going to be enough, no matter how bright and clever we are: I've met students who've graduated from theological college who still didn't have any revelation of the Kingdom and the spirit world.

It's this tiny thing again called "faith"! Faith is the germination of that little seed of revelation in the womb of our spirit. The Greek word for "seed" is "sperma" which indicates the life-giving power released when God's word is germinated by faith! It seems such a small thing, but it moves mountains! The old apostle John writes at the end of his life: "this is the victory that overcomes the world, even our faith!" Once our spirit has "seen" this and we have a "revelation" of who Jesus really is – not just head-knowledge – this faith makes us contagious. Revelation then opens to us the whole world of our sonship in Him, and this "overcomes the world". This is what Paul is talking about when he prays for the Ephesians church, that God would give them the spirit of wisdom and revelation, so that they would fully "see" the hope they are called to, the riches of their inheritance, and the incredible power available to those who simply believe. Somehow revelation gets you connected to

God himself. We "know" in our spirits, who we are in God and who God is in us. Each of us has to face this in our lives: "have I had a revelation yet, or is this just head knowledge?"

I passionately believe that this revelation comes as each believer is brought into a discipleship relationship which is more about obedience, than knowledge. Far more is then "caught" rather than "taught". The most viral command comes from Jesus himself, when he tells us to "make "disciples" in all people groups. This type of disciple cannot help but create other disciples, because they have been infected by the "heavenly virus" of His Kingdom. It is so simple, yet vast proportions of Churches today ignore His simple command.

CHAPTER 25

THE FINAL TRIGGER OF SACRIFICE, THAT LAUNCHES MOVEMENTS

COVENANTED BACK INTO THE WORLD TO SEEK AND SAVE THE LOST
Cross over from **Sin into "Sacrifice and Suffering"**

As we come to the *final stage of the Cross*, we now discover that we have come full circle, as in this stage we are covenanting our lives to be thrown back out into the stormy seas of humanity, to rescue people who are drowning, helping them to cling to the Cross as a life belt. In biblical terms we are living with a new passion to seek and save the "lost" by bringing them to embrace the Cross - laying our lives down to reach those who have no revelation of who Jesus is, and who are blindly hurtling towards an eternity without Him.

This is where we cross over from *"sin"* into *"sacrifice and suffering"* and this is where we cross back into the world. This may sound very counter intuitive: it seems we are going backwards into suffering! No, this is the whole upside-down nature of the Kingdom: Paul shouts out in Philippians 3:10: "I want to know Christ – yes, to know the power of His resurrection, *but also to share in the fellowship of His sufferings and become like Him in His death!"* It's a covenantal decision, as we cannot do this in our own strength. It is in our covenant with Him that we are enabled to cross back into the world and it inevitably embraces sacrifice and it embraces suffering. I know this is not an exciting uplifting word, but every believer since those early disciples, has had to face this call of God to be willing to embrace suffering and sacrifice. Let's see what apostle Peter says in 1 Peter 4:1: "Therefore since Christ suffered in his body, *arm yourselves also with the same attitude, because he who has suffered in his body is done with sin."*

Peter is saying: "listen, you must pick up this spiritual weapon - this will be your greatest weapon: arm yourselves with this attitude of sacrifice and suffering, because once you pick this up, you're done with sin and you're not going to mess around with sin anymore." If we embrace this same attitude as Jesus, then we are going to be militant in this world - there will be something contagious about us. We covenant our lives back into the global harvest fields, whether in the Nations or across the street: as we often hear, "it's not necessarily about crossing the sea, but it's essential to see the Cross". When we get a revelation of the Cross, we are willing to become broken bread for the world. Just like that young boy in the feeding of the 5000, we simply put the meagre offering of our lives into His all-powerful hands and He multiplies us to feed thousands!

We're saying to Father "I know I'm nothing: my life may represent just a few loaves and fishes, but I'm going to put all of me into your hands and I pray Father that you'll break me and miraculously multiply me to the feed the multitudes in the world"

An extraordinary thing happens when I just put "little me" into His hands, knowing that I am nothing special: we often feel that we look as ineffective as those meagre loaves and fishes. Yes, we're insignificant to the vast needs we see around us, but then suddenly we find that He begins to use us to touch other people's lives. We look back on our lives and realize that thousands and thousands of people have been "fed" through our lives! How on earth does that happen, that people are being fed by my life? What we long for is a viral multiplication of who we are and who He is, and that it explodes out into the world. We become His ambassadors with His love, power and authority and we know, "it's not me, but it's Christ in me, that is the hope of glory"; we're able to say "what I have, I give you" because we know that inside us we have something to give. Only a revelation of the Cross compels us to reach out to the "lost" like this.

Let me repeat here that suffering and sacrifice are so important, because Paul reminds us in Romans 12 that we must put our lives on the altar as a "living sacrifice": without sacrifice, there is no fire. Also, if you look at Romans 8, Paul says very clearly that the Holy Spirit gives us a deep inner witness that we are children of God and that we're heirs with God and co-heirs with Christ - *provided that we share in His sufferings so that that we can also share in His glory*: without suffering, there is no glory. These two statements ("without sacrifice there is no fire" and "without suffering there is no glory") are a classic description of the upside-down nature of God's kingdom.

In the same way, in the natural world, a virus only lives within a person while they're still alive, and once the host is dead, the virus very soon dies. However, God's kingdom is the exact opposite: the "heavenly virus" of God's contagious nature and power only comes alive in us when we embrace the death of Jesus on the Cross, and you and I "come to death". Paul says it in Galatians 2:20,

"I have been crucified with Christ, and I no longer live; the life I now live in this body, I live by faith in the son of God who loved me and gave Himself for me." If we are able to live embracing that death, His viral contagious life comes alive in us; but if "little me" fights to stay alive, it will kill that virus of the Kingdom operating through my life.

We have to recognize that something supernatural is happening here and that is why Paul says that "we are always carrying around in our body the death of Jesus so that the life of Jesus may also be revealed in our body." (2 Cor 4:11) Simply put, our death to ourselves produces life: "for we who are alive are always being given over to death for Jesus sake so that His life may be revealed in our mortal body. So then death is at work in us but life is at work in you." It's a very different type of message from Paul: it helps us understand that sacrifice is actually our greatest weapon, not our greatest failure. When we embrace this truth, we have effectively crossed over into "enemy territory" and our lives become gripped with a passion to rescue men, women and children from the devil's grip.

I worked for several years for the Chinese evangelist Brother Yun, who introduced himself to his captors as the "heavenly man". For him, Christian faith and ministry only begins with the decision to embrace a willingness to lay your life down to reach people who don't know Jesus. He was imprisoned, tortured and his legs smashed and broken so that he could never walk again. He was miraculously healed and managed to escape from prison by walking out past many security guards and found his way to Europe where he sought asylum in Germany.

He was unable to go back to China, but years later he began to work into Myanmar, where his reputation eventually caught the eye of the government and he was imprisoned again. With no fear for his life, each morning as all the inmates gathered outside squatting on the ground for daily Buddhist worship, he would leap to his feet and jump and dance and praise Jesus! This boldness and courage had such an impact on the inmates, that one by one they came to him and surrendered their lives to Jesus, and he "baptized" them with the only water he had from the washroom taps. After about six or seven months they had to throw him out of the prison and out of the country, as so many prisoners were becoming followers of Jesus! Now that is an example to how viral and contagious our lives can become once we are willing to embrace sacrifice and suffering.

So, let me just sum up the message of the cross in a few words: Jesus poured out His blood on the cross so that we could be rescued from the power of *"Satan, Sin and Self"*. He shouted in triumph "it is finished!" His Spirit and His blood seal an unbreakable covenant with us which guarantees us victory and freedom over the "world, the flesh and the devil". By faith in that covenant we are empowered to cross over from the dominion of darkness into the Kingdom of Light, without being neutralized, seduced, or intimidated by the "world" around us. We cross over *"into Christ, into his Body, and then back into the world"* to see others saved; we do this by choosing to cross over into His *"sonship"*, then into His *"service"* and then finally into His *"sacrifice and suffering"* so that we can be part of that viral contagious movement which is dedicated to "seek and save the lost": it brings us to have an encounter with Jesus and we come to personally embrace the Cross for ourselves.

We have looked carefully at these two different sides of the Cross, by looking at the "mercy side" which is all about "us" and our dreams and then by looking at the "grace side" which is all about Him and His Kingdom. One word of caution though at the same time, please keep in mind the incredible victory of the Cross: over the last 30 years the whole move of the Spirit through the Toronto and Pensacola revivals brought "Father's love" back into first place: there has been a wonderful move of the Spirit bringing our focus back onto Jesus, in recapturing "our first love". This cannot however take the place of being totally captured by "God's first love" which is always His love for "souls". We can sometimes become so taken up with our renewed intimacy with Jesus, that we lose our passion to win people to Jesus – "so heavenly minded that we are no earthly good"! People need the Lord, and we must develop a heart that burns with the same fire as God's heart, passionate about rescuing people.

We must not be like a "Jabez generation" which just wants the blessing, and tends to shrink back from embracing sacrifice and suffering - we see this in 1 Chron 4:10: here we read the profound prayer of Jabez (which God did answer) for God to bless him, extend his territory, and for no harm or pain to come on him: yes, God answers prayers like this, but my Bible says that in the new covenant we should rather seek to have "the same attitude which was in Christ Jesus." He made himself nothing, gave up all his rights, became a servant, and humbled himself "even to death on the Cross". Jesus embraced "sacrifice and suffering" even though He could have pleaded with God to rescue Him from the Cross. Why? He knew His journey was downwards first: the very reason He came down to earth and took on flesh, was so that He could finally destroy all the power of the devil through the Cross and rescue the whole of the humanity from Satan. Remember, just before the crucifixion, He actually prays to His Father, "Right now I am shaken. So what am I going to say? 'Father, get me out of this'? No, this is why I came in the first place!" (John 12:27 Message). He was gripped by His Kingdom purpose to lay His life down for us on the Cross.

We are called to take the same journey: it's a journey downwards, first in humility, repentance and confession, we embrace the Cross and only then are we raised to live and reign with Him. Yes, He wants to bless us, but please don't stop where this generation is constantly tempted to stop: we don't want this to be a Jabez generation that just wants the blessing: we must go beyond that. In Luke 12:49 Jesus says, "I've come to bring this fire on earth and how I wish it was already kindled." He is desperate to bring this fire back onto the earth, desperate to bring something of His power and His viral Kingdom back on earth, and for us to be totally immersed, infected and compelled by this "heavenly virus" of His Kingdom. He comes to infect us with His faith, His hope, and His love, but what a full-on battle it is!

Sadly, so much of the world system and religion seeks to kill our hope, together with our perseverance and endurance, through injecting his "anti-virus" into our world - all kinds of fears, disappointments, and offenses. It seeks to kill our faith and our inner drive to work in the Kingdom, through feeding us with unbelief, rationalism and with humanism. It seeks to kill our love, passion, and prayer which labour in the Kingdom, by injecting caution, political correctness and fear back into the Body. A defeated and divided Body will never be effective, and so the glory fades and we become sterile and uncontagious, condemned to live with a form of religion which denies the power of God. (2 Tim 3:5)

Don't forget however that we've read the end of the book and the Lamb wins! Be encouraged, God is never trumped by the enemy: the Cross wins every time! We may have lost so much, but we will recover all, because the devil is defeated. The simple choice we make to be willing to sacrifice and suffer to reach the lost, somehow triggers a movement of the Spirit that no man can stop. The viral Kingdom is released with power through the weapon of our sacrifice! This Kingdom anointing breaks the yoke that so many people live under: it breaks the chains of sin, fear and shame; it breaks the bondage of sickness and tormenting spirits in people's lives, and also releases people out of the terrible generational grip of poverty, triggering a fresh flow of love, grace and generosity in the people who are touched by the Kingdom.

CHAPTER 26

SOME KEYS OF THE KINGDOM

Before we come to the final chapter, let's look at this vital question: "what are some of the keys can we learn from these first apostles in the way we train a future generation of Kingdom warriors who will be involved in the battle for communities and nations?" There are so many, but let me address just seven keys:

Firstly *"Royal intercession"* is a key to a viral breakthrough: by this I mean Holy Spirit led prayer where we take God's commands seriously, in that He has given us the keys of the Kingdom and we need to use them. What is Royal Intercession? Well, intercession is made in our role as a priest, standing before God on behalf of people, but "Royal intercession" is believing that we are "seated" with Christ in heavenly places, and from His throne room we make decrees which change situations! God answers these declarations of faith which simply declare his Word into being. We are not pleading, we are declaring!

In Luke 11, Jesus teaches his new Kingdom leaders about four different levels of prayer:

1. The prayer of a child: the prayer of "intimacy"
2. The prayer of a covenant friend: the prayer of "intercession"
3. The prayer of a kingdom warrior: the prayer of "indignation"
4. The prayer of a son and heir: the prayer of "inheritance"

There is however a fifth level of prayer that Paul refers to in Romans 8, which I would call "birthing or travailing prayer". It is the type of prayer when the Holy Spirit comes on you and you pray/groan in the spirit as He Himself uses you as a mid-wife to help birth a move of God. This is not the forum for expanding on all this as it is a book in itself. (See "I love Prayer" by Rachel Hickson) However what we need to register is that "Royal intercession" comes when we know by faith, and beyond doubt, that we are His sons and heirs, and we begin to declare these decrees over our inheritance which is for Nations. Remember Peter fell asleep and couldn't even pray for one hour before the crucifixion! However, after the resurrection, Jesus breathes on them the spirit of prayer and then they prayed as son's who knew their father. They prayed in one place, in one accord, with one voice, and heaven came down and the whole building shook! This is "Royal intercession".

Secondly, *"reconciliation"* is a key to breakthrough: the devil will try every way to divide us, which is why reconciliation is so powerful. All the disciples were insecure and competitive: this caused fights, division, jealousy, and independence. Insecure leaders can end up crushing, controlling, bullying and wounding their people. Somehow the apostle John is secure and intimate with Jesus, and this is why Peter fights him, because he feels insecure. It takes those ten days locked up in the upper room to finally deal with this insecurity. It was as if Father God just treats the disciples like His children and says: "Now get upstairs and don't you come down until you've sorted this out!" I have no idea what happens behind those closed doors, but when the Holy Spirit has done what only He can do, they come out anointed and standing shoulder to shoulder! Peter had never worked with John before, but now they are inseparable. The reconciliation of relationships is essential to breakthrough, so we must never allow offences to separate us. Sometimes it is the act of reconciliation with the very person whom you have bounced off, that is the key to your breakthrough. This was the key for me in breaking through in Mombasa, Kenya, and the key in Watford, and Oxford in England,

and also the key in Medicine Hat in Canada – all these stories you will find in my book "Harnessed for Adventure!"

Thirdly, *"holiness"* is a key to breakthrough. It's not ours, but it's His holiness, and we begin to share and impart it as we allow Him to take us through times of discipline. However, we must beware of legalism concerning "holiness" as we are not trying to polish up our own holiness. This just leads to legalism, and it is very common after a move of God. Once we lose a passion for the lost, we can begin to navel-gaze and begin to dissect each other critically. Hebrews 12 says that God disciplines our self-life to develop us as "sons". The word used here means that we are no longer a toddler with temper tantrums looking no different from a non-Christian; we have by faith grown up into becoming mature "huios" sons of the Father, with the legal right to inherit the Kingdom. Sadly too few Christians grow up fully into "sonship" or as warriors. As "sons" we should expect persecution, in fact anyone who wants to lead a Holy, separated life in Christ, will be persecuted. (2 Tim 3:12) We must expect persecution, but then expect the Kingdom to advance as a result.

The fourth key is *"humility and transparency"* which is a key to breakthrough: we need to learn to serve each other just as Jesus washes their feet in John 13. Jesus breaks every rule and tradition and he models servant leadership. Peter can't cope with it and he over reacts. However, through the discipline Jesus puts him through, he does learn how to stop his independence and receive from others, and Peter finally learns to submit to the apostolic leadership of both James and Paul. Peter writes many years later that "God gives grace to the humble but opposes the proud"- it was from bitter experience. We must beware as leaders and stay transparent and accountable. Be prepared to look a fool for Christ, and don't be ashamed of the Gospel. I love the heart of David who dances with undignified passion, getting rid of every religious façade which was fueled by his pride and the fear of man. For David, this is the end of hiding his true call behind professionalism and status.

I will never forget the time in my leadership when I began to see the resurgence of panic attacks and PTSD as I stood up to preach. It had been 18 years since I had had a breakdown with PTSD in Northern Ireland when four of my soldiers had been killed. I had fully repented of the root of the fear of man in my life and had lived in faith and lived free for so many years. Years later however, I lost a battle of faith over a technicality, when I was seeking to take over a building with a 700-seater auditorium in Watford. As I retreated in shame, I "placed my faith on the back burner". It wasn't long before fear began to fill the vacuum and soon I was being gripped with panic attacks again.

Now in these circumstances, Kingdom leaders cannot hide and pretend. God is utterly good but remember that He also has to tell us some things which are not "nice" to hear! He told me to confess it to the church and get prayer to be free, but I was too proud to humble myself and be transparent. Three months later, my mother-in-law happened to be in the service, and God compelled me from my seat and said "Do it now! Confess to the church that you have been living in sin!" It was the most embarrassing moment as I confessed that I was being gripped by panic attacks and desperately needed them to pray for me. People rushed forwarded and bound every demon of fear and I was instantly free!

What I was not expecting however, was that this simple key of humility and transparency became a key to unlock the entire church, and suddenly the Spirit of God swept through our connect groups, enabling so many people to imitate me and confess the problems they were experiencing. It was a moment of freedom in so many lives. If we live "in the light", He truly will cleanse every area of sin and shame.

The fifth key is this: *"unconditional love"* is a key to breakthrough. It takes God's unconditional "agape" love to sustain and compel us, because so much of our love is fleshy, emotional and soulish. As a Church, we are not called just to be a social service: we are called to save souls. A social service can run on "filea" love which is soulish, flighty, relational, and fleshy, and changes with your circumstances. "Agape" is from the Spirit and this love perseveres through every trial and failure and never fails. We can almost hear Jesus saying to us today: "do you really "agape" me? Do you even "filea" me? Because I know how changeable you are with all your failures, but I have no one else: I need you to feed my sheep!"

As Paul says, "its only Christ's love that will compel us to seek the lost, because this convinces us that His blood is for every single person – no exceptions!" (2 Cor 5:14) I worked for years with a formerly aggressive Islamic Imam, who was dedicated to islamizing Africa through satellite media. He was certainly unlovable in this state, but a young YWAM girl was gripped with an "agape" love for him. She risked his wrath as she approached him and told him that he lacked real peace and needed to meet Jesus the Prince of Peace. He was furious and stormed off, but the word lodged in him. That night he unrolled his prayer mat in his hotel and asked Allah to tell him who was the Prince of Peace. He then had the most profound life-changing encounter with Jesus who came to him, and soon after this he surrendered his life to Jesus. Since that time, this one man has been responsible for countless Muslims being discipled through to Jesus in their living rooms as they watch his TV or internet programmes in Arabic, Urdu, Farsi and other languages. He is a true Kingdom warrior going where angels would fear to tread. To him, nothing is impossible with Jesus.

The sixth key is that *"anointing and authority over demons"* is a key to breakthrough. Only this will overcome demonic strongholds and opposition. Peter and the apostles come out of the upper room not only with power, but more essentially *with authority*. Pentecost was never just about the power to heal, because they could do that before they were even baptized in the Holy Spirit. These early miracles were purely by faith. This outpouring at Pentecost was far more about releasing onto them an authority over the demonic powers that were holding Jerusalem. Nothing can stop Peter now! The devil can't shut him up, destroy him or even imprison him.

Just like Brother Yun, the Heavenly Man, Peter just walks out of prison to the amazement of the local believers. Peter then leads the breakthrough in Jerusalem in which one third of the city is saved, with extraordinary signs and wonders, and with many demons being cast out. The whole Roman empire is impacted! It's time that we confront demonic strongholds in our cities, regions and nations. I know this is not popular and is highly controversial, but it's a vital key. Take it by faith or leave it and find yourself marginalized spiritually, unable to breakthrough even your local strongholds.

My spiritual father, Alan Vincent, was baptized in the Spirit as he sought God for a breakthrough in Bombay, India. He found himself battling with the demonic powers which controlled that area of Bombay. His revival prayer group grew smaller and smaller, but he would not give up. One night he found himself being physically attacked in bed by a demonic power with piercing eyes. As a Kingdom warrior, he was outraged with that "indignation" which comes from the Spirit, and he wrestled with the demon, bringing down a curtain rail, as this demonic presence literally "vanished" through the bars on his window. It was soon after this that the Kingdom broke through in Bombay, and tens of thousands of former Catholics had an encounter with Jesus and gave their lives to Christ.

In Argentina, I similarly met with a man called Omar Cabrera who would take a hotel room in a city and then humble himself through fasting and repentance, claiming the city for Christ. He would persist until invariably he was assaulted by a demonic power.

As he withstood these attacks and bound the principality of that city, thousands would then come to the Lord. I should also mention that as we sought God for one particular city, my Rachel was also attacked by a demonic figure which threatened her: "If you touch that city, I will kill you!" We are not playing games here. This is a matter of life and death as we seek God to advance His Kingdom globally. Do not fear though - Jesus has overcome the enemy and we are condemned to victory, provided we remain in Him!

This leads us to the seventh key of *"suffering and sacrifice"* which we talked about in the last chapter, and this is a major key to breakthrough – it is a powerful weapon. Power is released through faith, as well as through suffering and sacrifice, because the Cross has always been God's ultimate weapon, through which He disarmed every principality and power. I recall the words of that famous Rumanian pastor, who when threatened by the Government to be executed if he persisted in preaching about Jesus: "If you persist in threatening me with your ultimate weapon of taking my life, then you will force me to use my ultimate weapon, which is to lay my life down for Jesus. The only problem for you is that my weapon is a thousand times stronger than yours!" You can almost hear the Holy Spirit adding like Clint Eastwood: "Make my day!". It is so clear in Rev 12:11 that we overcome the devil through the Blood of Jesus, the word of our testimony, but most importantly, through our willingness to suffer and sacrifice our lives for the Kingdom. There is no defense against a spiritual army that has already laid down it's right to live. They are fearless, and unstoppable.

These seven simple keys are examples, and really just a few of the many Kingdom keys which Jesus has given us. The important thing to recognize as we close this chapter, is that we have already been given the keys of the Kingdom. Through them we have the authority to open situations and shut situations, to allow and disallow, to bind and loose. We have been given power over all the works of the enemy, and nothing by any means will harm us. We have been commanded to go as His representatives and be carriers of the Kingdom wherever we go - preaching about the Kingdom, healing the sick, raising the dead and casting out demons. Finally, we have his covenant commitment that He will be with us whenever we step out for the Kingdom. When we go, He goes; when we command, He commands. We are His Body, and we are inseparable from Him. His life is our life, and His victory is our victory.

In our day, all hell is being released to wipe out the Church, but God is turning it, so that when we are attacked in one direction, the devil will be made to flee in seven directions. In the western world, we are seeing an all-out attack on the Church, seeking to outlaw the wearing of crosses, display Christian posters, possess Christian views on sexual identity, gender identity, and even on marriage. However, it is often at such times that God always gathers His people in desperate prayer, and then explodes a revival to force the pendulum to swing. This has happened again and again over the last 500 years in Europe. Now as we head for 2033, the 2000th anniversary of the Cross, when the devil tried his hardest to kill the "heavenly virus", dark clouds are gathering against the Church - but God has a plan! Tighten your seat belts!

Isaiah 60 says that it's time to "arise and shine, because great darkness is over our western nations, but His light is on us for this unique time of history. The question is: "What are you personally looking at as a Kingdom leader? If you just look at the advancing clouds and persecution of the Church, with all the giants, the impossibilities and negatives, then you will be of little use to the Kingdom! Or are you one of those who can see in the invisible the massive harvest and awakening that we are stepping into. Only those who see in the invisible will attempt the impossible. As the Moravians shouted to each other as they sacrificed their lives to reach the lost, "the Lamb will receive the reward for His suffering!"

The end is not the end until God says it's "the end", and right now the challenge in our western nations is to join the faith of the Church in the Global South and believe that even our western nations can be saved. The God who mobilized the Chinese Back to Jerusalem movement, is serious about bringing the Kingdom light right through the Buddhist, Hindu, and Muslim nations. First like Abraham, we must face the facts that we are barren, and powerless in our own strength, but we must not fuel the fear and despair! We must learn from the apostles about the power of suffering, and the power of the Cross in Kingdom warfare.

Listen! God is looking for passionate radical followers who are willing to sacrifice! He hates lukewarmness and indifference and would rather that we are either hot or cold. He calls us not only to be baptized with the Spirit but also with His fire! Beware though, because fire will consume, test, and purify. It falls on the sacrifice of spiritual hunger and passion. In closing, may I plead with you that the altar is prepared: will you hear the cry in heaven, "Where are those who are willing to sacrifice? Where is the fire, the passion and the zeal?" He needs you and me to be carriers of this fire. We keep repeating, "No sacrifice - no fire! No suffering - no Glory!" Let's hear Elijah challenging us in 1 Kings 18:21, "how long will you waver with unbelief? If He's God give him everything! The God who answers by fire, He is your God!"

My life was dramatically changed through two encounters with the fire of God on May 25th 1994 and April 24th 2013. The first was an open vision of the fire of God sweeping through Muslim nations, and the second was God wrestling with me to believe Him for 30 million Muslims. These were my personal encounters, but I believe that our nations and our continent are in crisis and it's time for a showdown in the spirit: we all need a major encounter with God! The altar is prepared - but who is willing to lay their lives on the altar? Where are the Davids and Peters who've messed up, but have a true heart for God? Where are the Deborah's, the Ruth's, the Sampson's, the Elisha's, and the Elijah's? Who will carry the fire of God and this "heavenly virus" as a Kingdom leader today?

My final question is this: "how much of God do you want?" If you are really hungry and thirsty for God's Kingdom, don't let anyone or anything stop you. The reality in terms of numbers is that there were 500 people who had an encounter with Jesus immediately after He was raised from the dead. Of those 500, 380 were happy to go back to their old religious ways – that's about 75% who never pushed through to the Kingdom. Only 120 were hungry and passionate enough about the Kingdom, that they would not rest until they saw the Kingdom begin to operate through their ministry. We are praying for you that you will be one of those Kingdom leaders that blazes a trail of revival amongst this up and coming generation. "Father, let your Kingdom come!"

CHAPTER 27

PERSECUTION AND MARTYRDOM CANNOT STOP THE KINGDOM!

Now please bear with me, as I complete the story we began with at the beginning of this book: remember that I talked about Paul's encounter with God, which then launches him to take this good news of God's Kingdom around the known world. I'm fully aware that in Chapter 7, I did give a brief overview of the early history of breakthrough in Ephesus, but I feel this really needs repeating, so that we can allow the implications of history to fully connect with all that is happening today. Through repetition, I'm praying that this will burn in your soul!

I mentioned that Paul is desperate and plans to sweep right through the whole of Asia minor with the Gospel. Paul wants to travel all the way up to Ephesus and neutralize that demonic stronghold which ruled Asia Minor through the spirit of Artemis/Diana. However, we read in Acts 16 that when he tries to get into Asia, "the spirit of Christ stops him"- Jesus just stops him in his tracks and then takes Paul on a "walkabout", travelling through five different cities, to learn the keys of spiritual warfare. God is wrestling with his intellect because he hasn't yet come to understand the full realm of the Spirit. Paul has to come to understand the power and victory of the Cross, and I shared earlier how he grows in faith as God leads him through each of these cities.

Finally, major breakthrough comes, and he sees that the power of the Cross is really working through him. So, we come to Acts 19 and we watch in awe as one man, who understands the power of the Cross and the authority of the Kingdom, walks into Ephesus, the demonic HQ of Asia Minor. One man who is utterly contagious with this "heavenly virus" walks into town. A man who now understands the Cross and has the glory of "sonship, service, and sacrifice" pulsing within his veins. He is literally a reflector of the full glory of the Kingdom of God; one man walks into the city and all hell begins to tremble and flee, and all of heaven breaks loose into the city; one man brings the Kingdom "heavenly virus" to Ephesus, and the rest is history! It is an extraordinary revival: the witches and the warlocks and every other demonic emissary throw all their witchcraft items out into the streets, terrified because God has come to town.

They burn millions of pounds worth of witchcraft objects and resources, and the glory of God breaks through. Even Paul's shadow heals people, and the power of God just breaks loose because one man understands the full power of the Cross and what it has accomplished. This single breakthrough starts a mega battle for Europe and a mega battle for Asia - two different spiritual territories.

In the same way, in Luke 3 and 4 we see hell unleashing an extraordinary outpouring of demonic power against Jesus, as He steps into His sonship at age 30; as He comes up out of the Jordan the Holy Spirit comes upon Him, and for the first time in human history, a man is standing on earth knowing that He has been given all power in heaven and on earth. The alarm bells go off in hell, and the devil tries every way to rob Jesus of His confidence in the power and authority of His sonship.

This moment in Ephesus with Paul is identical: now the contagious Kingdom of God that is resting on Paul spreads virally throughout the Body of Christ as they step into the revelation and confidence of their sonship in Christ. As an instant reaction, all of hell breaks loose to stop the Body of Christ working in its sonship and in its power and authority. So, the enemy unleashes unbelievable persecution against the church in AD64. Much of the city of Rome is burned down, and the Emperor Nero blames the Christians: thousands and thousands of Christians are burnt. They are martyred for their faith: some are dipped in tar and just used as flaming candles around the temples and orgies of the day- it is just horrific. It is unbelievable carnage as the enemy comes in to destroy the church. In AD70, Jerusalem is destroyed, and the temple is totally dismantled: every single one of the apostles is killed, and Peter is just about to be martyred.

I'm telling you this for one reason: it looked then as if the devil had won, but God was just getting started! We are in a similar position in many nations: we are stepping into a time of serious persecution of true believers. (Religious people will not be targeted, but true Bible believing spirit-filled believers will come under significant attack.) In AD 70 it looks as if the devil has won: the kingdom of darkness seems to have triumphed and there are only a few weak remnants struggling to survive.

This is the background to Peter's apostolic letter when he boldly says, "Come on, listen! I want you to really understand this: I want you to pick up an incredibly powerful weapon that you don't realize that you possess: "arm" yourself with this same attitude as Jesus - be willing to sacrifice and suffer for doing what is right and pleasing to God - this will prove effectively that you are done with sin, and all its domination in your life, and that you are committed to spend the rest of your life doing the will of God." As Peter writes this letter, it releases an unshakeably bold faith through those remnant believers because he is convinced with renewed Kingdom faith, that all their Old Testament prophecies are going to happen. He is convinced that the Kingdom of God is about to break through; he is convinced that Jesus is going to come in mighty power; he is convinced that the reign of God is going to start to breakthrough against all the demonic attacks being thrown at them. Something is about to break through, but it is going to take a lot longer than Peter estimates, and he will be martyred before it all happens.

In AD68, four years after the persecution begins, the apostle John himself comes to Ephesus. He takes over the apostolic leadership from Peter who has been martyred and John leads the church in Ephesus for 12 years: he still doesn't break through, and he is arrested and is sent off to Patmos Island. Dark clouds are gathering over the whole of the known world and he writes a letter to the body of Christ with a message direct from heaven. In Revelations 2, God says through him, "listen, Church in Ephesus, I know your hard work and perseverance; I know you can't tolerate wicked people, and you've had to sort out a few false prophets. Yes, you've persevered and endured hardships for me, but I'm holding one thing against you: you have lost the love you had at first."

So began 30 years of the most horrific crucifixion of the church - unbelievable carnage. I have to say that I believe that we are even now about to see the same unbelievable carnage within the Body of Christ: I think we're about to go through some really rough times in western nations, just as is happening in the global south where Christians are regularly being martyred for their faith.

As I said before, it's a sad fact that in many places in western nations, the body of Christ has been focusing on recapturing its first love again, but we've lost His first love which is "souls being saved". Our first love is Him, but His first love has a different focus: He died for the whole world, and over 40% of the world is still unreached by the gospel. We must catch hold of His first love which is for souls, and then be contagious ourselves and influence every believer with this passion for souls. It's time to grab hold of the Cross now in our spirits and persevere through all the trials; it's time to be absolutely unflinching and unswerving, knowing that the devil is defeated!

The dark clouds of secularism, atheism and Islam are gathering over England, Europe, and the States, and much of the western world, and the church is feeling the early waves of what will become intense persecution. What the devil doesn't understand though, is that when he makes the mistake of crucifying Jesus, this actually releases an incredibly viral power out into the world which destroys the dominion of darkness and his demonic control. The Cross of Christ releases freedom, life, and healing! In the same way, when the devil seeks to crucify the church through intense persecution, this actually triggers them to use the time-tried weapons of sacrifice and suffering, which eventually overcomes all the powers of darkness.

For those 30 years from AD 64 to AD95 an unbelievable demonic power is released that spreads right through the known world. During his years of exile in Patmos, John has come to faith in the power of the gospel, and the authority he has against all demonic spirits. What happens in AD95 is that John, probably about 90 years old, is released from Patmos and he comes back to Ephesus: he walks into the temple of Artemis/Diana and he confronts that demonic presence up at the altar: *the altar splits in two, and half the temple just falls down.*

You couldn't invent such a scenario: this actually happens and is recorded in history. From that moment it was all over for the demonic principalities within Europe, and the cult of Artemis/Diana dies out. Within 50 years there is hardly even a trace of it, and Ephesus becomes the centre of the advancement of God's Kingdom for 200 years. *The power of God just explodes over the whole of Europe for the next 200 years: this is the viral Kingdom I am praying for!*

This same pattern can be traced in revival history: we read of horrific spiritual attacks which end up paving the way several decades later for a revival breakthrough. One example of this is China:

this is exactly what happens in China in 1949 when Mao Zedong is swept into power: every Bible is burned, every pastor is either killed or sent to a labour camp, and every church is closed. There is a total crucifixion of the Body of Christ in China for 30 years from 1950 to 1980. The enemy always feels that he has achieved "checkmate", but God is just getting warmed up! The devil just does not understand the activity of the Holy Spirit: he tries to remove every trace of the Christian faith but cannot remove the presence of the Holy Spirit from the hearts of faithful believers.

Within those 30 wilderness years, there is an invisible movement of the Spirit at the grass roots level, with believers secretly praying and weeping for God's Kingdom to breakthrough. They pray in caves, in the forest and in the mountains and fields. Everything on the surface looks as if the devil has won: but suddenly in the 1980's, the spirit of God explodes into a visible movement of revival which is unstoppable by the Government. (If you haven't read "The Heavenly Man", it is essential reading to understand the miraculous move of revival and the cost that many paid) Over the next 50 years the Body of Christ grows from what it was in 1950 (800,000 Christians) up to 80 -100 million believers. The "heavenly virus" is released again into the church, and even today with the current regime trying to stamp out the Church, it is unstoppable.

In the Church of Jesus Christ, we may have to go through that same "crucifixion experience" to bring us back to the same viral form of Christianity of those early disciples. We are praying that this will not happen, but it may well have to happen to some groups of believers in the next few years: we too might have to go through that "crucifixion experience" here in Europe and in the western world, before we finally get to see that viral form of Christian faith which will sweep not only through Europe but throughout the world.

As we come to a close, let's read one final scripture: Hebrews 12:2 "Let us fix our eyes on Jesus, the author and perfecter of our faith, who for the joy set before him endured the Cross, scorning its shame and sat down at the right hand of the throne of God." This is all about fixing our eyes on Jesus. Once we stop looking into our shadow, and we turn and fix our eyes on Jesus, He begins our journey of faith; but what is so fantastic is that He's also committed to finish and complete our faith journey. It all begins when we put our total trust in what Jesus accomplished on the Cross: this activates and releases the power of Kingdom faith in each of us, which then guarantees that there is a great joy of harvest ahead of us.

There is an incredible harvest that is happening right now somewhere in our globe. God's harvest fields are ripe and ready for harvest at different times. I have personally witnessed the ripe harvest fields in Africa and Asia during my time directing Reinhard Bonnke's Crusades. God has a perfect time to harvest in every Nation and Continent. We need however to understand from both our story of the battle for Ephesus in Paul's day, and our battle for China in this modern era, that persecution and revival often flow together. Right now, as we well know, persecution is happening across North Africa, but people are coming to Christ in huge numbers. I could name many other places across the world that are also experiencing persecution. Let's believe for the same harvest in all these places. Watch out for the revival that Hudson Taylor prophesied back in 1889, coming across Russia, and impacting all of Europe. All the current suffering of the Russian people under the current brutal regime, is creating an environment which is perfect for revival fires.

Revival often follows persecution, which is why we too need to endure the Cross: there will be persecution. Paul was writing to the Church in Ephesus, and He tells them that because of the Cross, God has raised us up with Christ, to be seated comfortably with him in the heavenly realms, knowing the devil is defeated: no matter what the devil is doing, we look from our vantage point, seated together with Christ, knowing that Jesus holds all power and authority and that this is the place where we really belong.

The Cross has won the day: we are a victorious people. It doesn't matter what the devil tries to do to us; he may try to obliterate us; he may try to oppress us; he may throw law cases against us and try to silence and marginalize the church. Yes, we are going to get all hell thrown at us and suffer persecution for our faith: this is guaranteed biblically to anyone who wants to live a holy life in Christ Jesus; but we are condemned to victory if we remain in Christ because of the power of the Cross.

The devil cannot stop what is about to happen across Europe, or across the Islamic nations. God's plans for the America's, Asia, Africa and Australia cannot be thwarted by the enemy. We are praying that you will come to faith in the full completed work of the Cross, and that you will be one of those who responds to heavens call: you can almost imagine a sign raised up for every man and woman to read: "Wanted! The Kingdom needs empty, broken lives – people who are willing to embrace the Cross and willing to lay their lives down to see His Kingdom come!" God is calling for this army of volunteers, who have had the revelation that they are crucified with Christ and they no longer live, but Christ and His power live within them. There is no defence against an army of "Kingdom warriors" who are dead to themselves.

Let me pray for you:

"Father, I want to thank you for this time together with my friend and thank you for this challenge as we looked at the full spectrum of the journey of the Cross. I pray that we would be those who do embrace the Cross by faith and are then willing to cross over into all the fullness of our sonship, learning to serve within the body, as well as to be sent out into the harvest fields of the world, ready to sacrifice and suffer with you. Oh, Father, what a salvation! But, oh what a destiny and what an inheritance! My God, let there be a spirit of wisdom and revelation which grips each one of us. Let us come to such a place of praise, with our eyes fixed on

you, knowing how victorious you are. Our God is a victorious God! We are condemned to victory provided we remain in Christ, because of the power of that Cross."

Thank you for completing this journey with us: I know that you may well need to spend time meditating on each stage of the Cross until you know that you have appropriated all that Jesus won for you through His sacrifice. Let's be like Paul when he was shut up in prison: he just decided to praise God late into the night, and this was the key to him walking out into freedom. Many of you may well be going through similar painful situations and difficult times: so please, let's fix our eyes on Jesus and just begin to praise Him. There is such earth-shattering and prison-shattering faith that bubbles up when we begin to praise him daily. Praise Him even when it's all going wrong. Just praise Him for all He has won for us on the Cross, and let's keep on asking for this revelation of the Cross to break loose in and through our lives. Let's make God's love go viral! God bless you!

APPENDIX 1:

BROTHER YUN ON THE CHURCH IN CHINA

Morrison was the earliest person to translate the Bible into Chinese. However, I felt Hudson Taylor and China Inland Mission influenced China in an even greater way; Hudson Taylor's emphasis was not only on reaching the coastal areas, but also inner China. In the 1920s the Chinese Church began to have a structure. The characteristics of the church of Watchman Nee in Shanghai, and MingDao Wang in Beijing, greatly influenced the lives of the CHC (Chinese House Church) Leaders in the 70 – 90s. MingDao Wang's controversial teaching on Culture and Christianity had a great emphasis on a Holy Lifestyle. There are not many members of MingDao Wang's church today, and it does not influence today's church in a great way, however people do remember them, because they were against the 'Three Self Movement', insisting on the Holiness of the church. The fruit of their perseverance has lasted until today. Watchman Nee's theology on spirituality and a devoted life has been adopted by the Chinese House Church and influenced the CHC for decades.

The formation of the family style church of Watchman Nee, introduced the style of parental church management. From the 80s until the present day, the Western Church has participated in and co-operated with the Missions Vision God gave to the Chinese Church: to take the Gospel 'Back to Jerusalem". Their mutual understanding is: "Lift up the Bible. Fulfil the Great Commission. Lift up the Word of God." They emphasize living a devout and holy life, and also evangelism and the work of the Spirit. Personally, I feel this has had the greatest impact and contribution to the Chinese Church.

These past decades, China has had two types of church: one is the government recognised 'Three Self Patriotic' (TSP), which includes the 'Christian Council Church' and the other, is the Chinese House Church. The latter did not register with the government, so it is therefore not recognised by the government. Since they are free from Governmental control, they are also known as the 'underground church'; this group of Chinese House Church leaders are people of prayer, people with a vision and a mission, and most of all, they are willing to pay the price with their lives for the gospel of Jesus Christ to continue to advance with viral speed.

They are zealous, because they want to fan the fire of evangelism. Today, the emergence of a third type of church: the "registered church", affiliated with the TSP, has become the City Professional Church. We do thank God for his wonderful plan: since the 1979 revolution, God has slowly opened the door of China. Many visiting scholars have overseas experience, and at the same time, many visiting scholars and professors enter Chinese universities. This trend has provided a platform for evangelism and benefited the mission movement. Many were converted overseas, and those who visited China have converted many too. Those who were converted overseas have returned and are beginning to start up gospel meeting points in China.

Through prayer, China slowly began to open up, though now there has been a huge escalation of government control through a massive Intelligence network, which makes it almost impossible for foreign missionaries to work secretly within China. Having said that, when we anticipate the development of the church, do not put much weight on the promises the government has given the Chinese House Church Movement. The reason is that our Christian faith does not build on what the government promises, but builds on the precious word of God, which never changes. Praise God: with China opening her door to the world, many missionaries have secretly entered rural China, evangelising, healing, casting out demons and bringing forth a great revival within rural Chinese House Churches. The most obvious revival has been in He-nan, An-hui and Shang-dong areas. In those areas, one baptism service could have a thousand baptism candidates!

CHC leaders face imprisonment for Christ, yet many prisoners' lives have been changed by the love of Christ. Over the last 40 years, with this kind of leadership carrying such a contagious 'heavenly virus', the Gospel is spreading, and it is far more effective than any human virus! However, I do believe that the greatest impact is yet to come. China has experienced many revivals. The working of the Holy Spirit is at its first stages. I see that Jesus is raising up the younger generation, just like his servants Joshua and Caleb, and they will cause China to experience even greater glory and revival.

Truly, the future of the Chinese Church is to fulfil world mission by facing these six mission fields: the atheist world regardless of race, the Buddhist world, the Hindu world, the Muslim world, the Jews and the Western world and America.

I totally believe that the Lord has called China to be a great Mission Nation. If a church only concerns itself with its own internal affairs, then it will lose sight of the bigger picture. It will be stuck on minor things and gets absorbed with inner affairs; but we are called to serve God with faith, and the first priority is Missions. When we start this, God grants us all we need. It is like the days of old, when the Israelites crossed the River Jordan: the minute we step into the River Jordan, God will cause the river to stop.

In the Chinese House Church, Praise and Worship is so unique; "neither on the mountain, nor in the temple," but they worship God "in spirit and truth". Regardless of gender or age, each person longs to be used by God, and they preach with boldness the Gospel of the Kingdom. They often gather in two's or three's to pray at home; Bible Studies meet in places of work and testify for Jesus. In these ways many 'house church', fellowships and teams are formed.

The Chinese House Church's vision and mission is to do mission cross-culturally. They are willing to go to places where human nature makes us reluctant to go, going where the gospel has yet to be heard, reaching the unreached, such as the Arab world. This is our vision.

A few years ago, some brothers and sisters from South Korea accepted the challenge of becoming martyrs for the sake of the gospel. At the time, I was preaching in Afghanistan. God's Spirit came on me as I was preaching, and with boldness I pleaded with the body of believers there to intercede for these Koreans; the result was that all of them were released! So we see that the Muslim world is not a place which is beyond our reach. In the context of mission, the Chinese have so many advantages: for instance, the Chinese believers have grown and matured through really oppressive experiences, and so we are flexible and can adjust to extreme situations; Chinese food is diverse, so we're able to adapt to various food; Chinese language skills are strong.

My constant prayer is that the Chinese House Churches will step out into mission. Mission does not replace the need for the establishment of new churches, but it does motivate church growth. The aim of Church is "Mission" - Churches should be founded in it. Therefore, I propose that we create "mission-motivated" Churches. My preaching in the Western World is to plead with Christians to take a new Kingdom approach: to break from selfish, individualistic and self-centred Christianity. I believe this is the only route the Western Church should adopt, in order to recover its health.

It is so essential and important that Christians are salt and light in the society. The Church vision must be "mission"; taking the Gospel of Jesus Christ through every Nation on earth, especially those closed nations – all the way "Back to Jerusalem". We are commanded to "make disciples of all nations". If you are willing to be used by God, then be obedient to the Great Commission; be committed to mission, receiving the baton of mission and taking the gospel to the ends of the earth. This is the vision, and something that the Chinese House Churches have embraced in the past but need to keep alive into future.

The Chinese House Churches have a challenging future ahead and they so appreciate your prayers. In the past, evangelists and CHC leaders had to face years of anxiety and attacks. Poverty, crippling lack of resources, and an environment which is hostile to living faith, have all tested true believers in their love for Christ. Whatever the situation, they are faithful and loyal in service; they pray in all things and persevere in difficulty. Following the city economic development, resulting in urbanisation and materialism, the rich and poor gap is growing, and this affects the church too. Many small churches cannot afford to support their pastors. Thank God, some urban and coastal churches and some overseas churches are willing to support the ministries of poor churches; this includes the training of workers, spiritual materials and resources, and supporting the living allowance of pastors, etc. Helping these churches to maintain this support is so vital.

Please also pray for CHC leaders and pastors; many CHC leaders are facing immense political pressure, as they refuse to work with the TSP authority. In many locations, where the policy and local authority is repressive, the CHC is faced with even more pressure and persecution. The greatest pressure, however, which impacts them all, is the ever-growing wealth of China, her materialism, capitalism and secularism. The CHC underground church is also facing the influence of the occult and occult viruses.

Therefore, as the churches are facing all kinds of impacts, it is important and vital to be grounded in Biblical truth, especially systematic bible teaching; by helping these believers to have complete Biblical teaching, they develop the ability to distinguish secularism, aim for sanctification, be witnesses for Christ Jesus, and fight against the occult and false teaching. Churches are called and set aside to be holy. Persevere and hold on to the vision and mission to the end, bringing the Gospel "Back to Jerusalem". Be shining lights and witnesses for Jesus Christ.

Pray that the Holy Spirit will protect the church of China in this season, and that all the wonderful promises given, will be fulfilled. Let the "Heavenly Virus" spread like wild-fire.

The Bible said: 'I AM coming soon. Hold on to what you have, so that no one will take your crown.' (Rev 3:11)

– "Heavenly Man"- Brother Yun

APPENDIX 2:

Postscript by Pastor Surprise Sithole, Founding Member and International Director of Pastors for Iris Ministries

In 1986, at the age of 17, I had the privilege of being a part of an event Gordon Hickson organized for Reinhard Bonnke. I was one of more than 50,000 individuals that joined together in worship and pursuit of God's Kingdom that day. Its impact was immeasurable. I witnessed the power of God's love touch thousands of hearts simultaneously leaving an indelible mark on my life. Gordon Hickson's ability to mobilise such a massive crowd and create an atmosphere of spiritual awakening was truly extraordinary and blessed me so much..

This book, "Make God's Love go Viral", will uplift your spirit, inspire your faith, and fill your heart with joy. You will be left feeling renewed and inspired to spread God's love to everyone you encounter.

From the very first page, Gordon's writes with such infectious joy, drawing you in and inviting you to embark on a transformative journey. With each chapter, he effortlessly weaves together stories, anecdotes, and Biblical teachings to create a tapestry of love, kindness, and compassion. It's impossible not to be moved by his words and the profound impact they can have on your life.

One of the most remarkable aspects of "Make God's Love Go Viral" is its ability to resonate with readers, from all walks of life.

Whether you're a long-time believer, a sceptic searching for answers, or someone who simply wants to deepen their connection with God, this book has something for everyone. Gordon's message of love and acceptance transcends boundaries and reminds us all of the beauty and power of our shared humanity.

What sets this book apart from others is Gordon's genuine and infectious passion for spreading God's love. His words leap off the page and into your heart, igniting a fire within you to make a difference in the world. You'll find yourself eagerly turning the pages, hungry for more of Hickson's wisdom and guidance on how to become a vessel of God's love.

"Make God's Love Go Viral" is not just a book to be read and put aside; it's a call to action. Hickson challenges us to step out of our comfort zones and be the hands and feet of Jesus in a world that desperately needs love and compassion. With practical advice and heartfelt encouragement, he equips us with the tools to make a lasting impact in our communities and beyond.

In a world filled with negativity and division, "Make God's Love Go Viral" is a beacon of hope and inspiration. It reminds us that even the smallest acts of kindness can create a ripple effect that reaches far beyond our imagination. This book is a must-read for anyone seeking to make a difference and spread God's love in a world that so desperately needs it.

So, if you're ready to experience the joy of God's love in a profound and life-changing way, I wholeheartedly recommend "Make God's Love Go Viral" by Gordon Hickson. Prepare to be uplifted, inspired, and equipped to make a difference in the world. Let's join together and make God's love go viral!

ABOUT HEARTCRY FOR CHANGE

We work with churches and people from many nations and denominations to equip them in the following areas:

- **PRAYER** – Training an army of ordinary people in prayer schools and seminars to become confident to break the sound barrier and pray informed, intelligent and passionate prayers.

- **PROPHETIC** – Equipping the Church to be an accurate prophetic voice in the nation by teaching in training schools and conferences the principles of the prophetic gift. We seek to train people who are passionate to know the presence of God, are available to hear His voice, and then learn to speak His word with accuracy so that lives can be touched and changed.

- **WOMEN** – Delivering a message of hope to women across the nations and cultures to help them arise with a new confidence so that they can be equipped and ready to fulfil their destiny and execute their kingdom purpose.

- **CAPITAL CITIES** – Standing in the capital cities of the world, working with government institutions, businesses and the Church and then crying out for a new alignment of the natural and spiritual government in these places. A cry for London and beyond.

- **BUSINESS & FINANCE** – Connecting business people with their kingdom purpose so that provision can partner more effectively with vision and accelerate the purpose of God in nations. Connecting commerce, community and church for change!

- **LEADERS OF TOMORROW** – Mentoring and encouraging younger leaders to pioneer the next move of God in the areas of politics and government, social action and justice issues, creative arts, media and the ministry.

- » **NATIONS** - Partnering with nations, like Moldova, by supplying teaching, training and practical resources to strengthen and resource them as they work for breakthrough in their nations.
- » **SOCIAL MEDIA** - To be a regular voice of hope and encouragement through social media, via YouTube and Facebook. Providing regular teaching on relevant topics to help people keep their perspective in their everyday life.
- » **RESOURCES & CONFERENCES** - Writing books, manuals and training materials that will equip the church prophetically. Hosting Legacy Days where leaders and church members can be refreshed and refocussed in the presence of God.

HEARTCRY FOR CHANGE UK
CMS House,
Watlington Rd,
OXFORD,
OX4 6BZ
www.heartcry.co.uk
www.heartcryforchange.com

HEARTCRY FOR CHANGE USA
c/o Rainier Hills Christian Fellowship
23711 Entwhistle Rd E
Buckley
WA 98321
www.heartcry.us

FOLLOW RACHEL AND THE TEAM ON FACEBOOK

www.facebook.com/Heartcryforchange

OTHER BOOKS WRITTEN BY GORDON AND RACHEL HICKSON

RACHEL HAS WRITTEN 13 BOOKS:

- » Supernatural Communication, the Privilege of Prayer,
- » Supernatural Breakthrough, The Heartcry for Change,
  – PUBLISHED BY NEW WINE MINISTRIES.

- » Stepping Stones to Freedom,
- » Pathway of Peace,
- » Run your Race.
- » Eat the Word, Speak the Word
  – PUBLISHED BY MONARCH

- » Eat the Word Study Guide,
- » Supernatural Communication Study Guide,
- » Release My Frozen Assets
- » Eat the Word, Speak the Word - 2nd Edition
- » I Love Prayer
- » Spiritual Architects
- » Hope Filled
  – PUBLISHED BY HEARTCRY FOR CHANGE

GORDON HAS WRITTEN ONE OTHER BOOK:

- » Harnessed for Adventure, A personal story of our lives
  – PUBLISHED BY HEARTCRY FOR CHANGE

HOW TO ORDER OTHER BOOKS

Heartcry for Change published titles can be purchased through our website: www.heartcryforchange.com/shop in paperback and e-book formats.

Harnessed for Adventure is also available as an audiobook. Payment can be made in GBP £ or USD $ using a debit or credit card or PayPal.

All of the books are also available on Amazon.

Printed in Great Britain
by Amazon